D1566801

HANK GREENBERG
IN 1938

HANK GREENBERG IN 1938

HATRED AND HOME RUNS IN THE SHADOW OF WAR

RON KAPLAN

SPORTS
PUBLISHING

Sports Publishing books may be purchased in bulk at special discounts for sales promotion, corporate gifts, fund-raising, or educational purposes. Special editions can also be created to specifications. For details, contact the Special Sales Department, Sports Publishing, 307 West 36th Street, 11th Floor, New York, NY 10018 or sportspubbooks@skyhorsepublishing.com.

Sports Publishing® is a registered trademark of Skyhorse Publishing, Inc.®, a Delaware corporation.

Visit our website at www.sportspubbooks.com.

10 9 8 7 6 5 4 3 2 1

Library of Congress Cataloging-in-Publication Data is available on file.

Jacket design by Tom Lau
Front cover and spine photograph courtesy of the National Baseball Hall of Fame Library, Cooperstown, NY

Print ISBN: 978-1-61321-991-1
Ebook ISBN: 978-1-61321-992-8

Printed in the United States of America

This book is dedicated to the memories of Hank Greenberg, Jackie Robinson, and all the other pioneering athletes who battled to succeed for themselves and their communities in the face of prejudice and narrow-mindedness.

A NOTE ON STATISTICS

Prior to the sabermetric explosion popularized by Bill James, baseball relied on "traditional" statistics that may not stand the test of time when evaluating a player's accomplishments. Where possible, I have tried to include the newer generation of stats in an attempt to bear out Hank Greenberg's accomplishments.

TABLE OF CONTENTS

"It was 1938 and I was now making good as a ballplayer. Nobody expected war, least of all the ballplayers. I didn't pay much attention to Hitler at first or read the front pages, and I just went ahead and played. Of course, as time went by, I came to feel that if I, as a Jew, hit a home run, I was hitting one against Hitler."

—*Hank Greenberg: The Story of My Life*

PREFACE

_____

"It drove me to do better. To prove that a Jew could be a ballplayer."

—Hank Greenberg[1]

While taking a break from writing this book, I happened to come across *Sullivan's Travels* on Turner Classic Movies. How appropriate, I thought. The screwball comedy was particularly popular during the Great Depression. The genre usually depicted the difference between the salt-of-the-earth types who were down on their luck and the well-to-do who might have good intentions but were often socially oblivious. This 1941 feature, written and directed by the great Preston Sturges, told the tale of John L. Sullivan (not the boxer), a famous Hollywood director who was tired of making entertaining but basically throwaway fluff with such ersatz titles as *So Long, Sarong* and *Ants in Your Pants of 1939*.

"I want [the next] picture to be a commentary on modern conditions. Stark realism. The problems that confront the average man," Sullivan tells a couple of studio execs. "I want this picture to be a document. I want to hold a mirror up to life. I want this to be a picture of dignity! A true canvas of the suffering of humanity!" They counter with the suggestion that he should just make another of his wonderful—and profitable—musicals.

"How can you talk about musicals at a time like this, with the world committing suicide. With corpses piling up in the street, with grim death gargling at you from every corner, with people slaughtered like sheep," he steams.

"Maybe they'd like to forget," was their profound reply.

They remind Sullivan that he was brought up in the ranks of privilege, with boarding schools, sprawling mansions, and a financially stable and fulfilling life. How did he think he was qualified to comment on the problems of the common man?

A determined Sullivan takes up the challenge, naively believing he can just go to the wardrobe department, find some shabby clothes, set out with a dime in his pocket, and hit the rails. Armed with this new insight, he vows to return and create his masterpiece.

He embarks on his travels, albeit never too far ahead of the entourage his concerned bosses have tasked with taking care of him and making sure he doesn't get into too much trouble.

At first he is moved by what he finds, but circumstances change dramatically in the third act (no spoilers here) and he comes to see the light. Regardless of his noble intentions, he winds up back at the drawing board, humbled and relieved of hubris.

"There's a lot to be said for making people laugh," he concedes in the final scene when he is reunited with "his" people, all the wiser for his experiences. "Did you know that that's all some people have? It isn't much, but it's better than nothing in this cockeyed caravan."

In a sense, the Depression was a great equalizer. Poverty made brothers and sisters out of millions of people regardless of race, creed, or religion. On the other hand, it also opened the door for hatred, as some found it necessary to find a group to blame for the ills that had befallen this great nation. Anti-Semitism was rampant during that era, both in the United States and abroad. Adolf Hitler came to power at a time when Germany was still trying to get past its shameful defeat during the First World War and pointed to the Jews as a main reason their Fatherland was in such dire straits.

Meanwhile, in Detroit—where the New York–born Hank Greenberg had chosen to make his living playing baseball with the Tigers—hate-mongers like automobile tycoon Henry Ford and Catholic radio personality Father Charles Coughlin also decided it was the fault of the avaricious Jews that the world was going to hell in a handbag. Ford went so far as to publish an edition of *The Protocols of the Elders of Zion*, a pamphlet originally released in Russian as "proof" of a Jewish plan for global domination.

Given all this, it seemed somewhat surprising that Greenberg did not mention Ford in his memoirs outside a minor reference to the car company for which he worked during the off-season.

But according to Mark Rosengren in his excellent book *Hank Greenberg: Hero of Heroes*, Ford was just the type to cheerfully announce that some of his best friends were Jewish, especially when it could do him some good, either financially, socially, or politically.

> Ford liked Hank. Perhaps this is why Greenberg agreed to work for the company. . . . The affection might have blinded Hank to the reality of [Ford's] prejudice. Hank had heard the ethnic slurs on the field, but at other times people treated him well because he was a star ballplayer. "I don't think Hank realized how horrible anti-Semitism sometimes was because even Jew-haters wanted to shake his hand," his second wife, Mary Jo, said.[2]

We don't know what it was exactly that Greenberg did for the Ford Motor Company or for how long. Rosengren reports that the ballplayer listed his off-season employment on his military documentation as working in the personnel department for which he received $5,000 "to investigate subversive activities of individuals against the company."[3] That Greenberg would take on that kind of position, or that the company would entrust such a responsibility to a temporary employee, seems a bit far-fetched. Easier to believe is that this was the type of position for which Greenberg was used as window dressing, for the publicity.

Just like the movies, baseball is a part of the entertainment industry. It gives people the chance to unwind for a few hours, to forget their troubles. And when someone like a Babe Ruth or Hank Greenberg arrives on the scene—a player who can give a little extra jolt when it comes to doing things few had every accomplished—well, that's just gravy, mister.

Greenberg and the Tigers started out slowly in 1938, but by the middle of the season he was hitting home runs at a pace comparable to the 60 Ruth smashed out eleven years earlier. The "Big Bam" was the most exciting player of his generation and now here comes someone—a *Jew*, no less—to challenge the mark. That gave fans in Detroit, and eventually around the country, that respite to which Sturges alluded in his movie: It may not have been much, but it was better than nothing.

Notes

1. Ira Berkow, "The Plot Against Greenberg?" *Jewish Jocks: An Unorthodox Hall of Fame*, edited by Franklin Foer and Marc Tracy (Twelve, 2012), p. 65.
2. John Rosengren, *Hank Greenberg: The Hero of Heroes* (NAL, 2014), pp. 141–42.
3. Ibid, p. 142.

INTRODUCTION: IN THE BEGINNING . . .

"Hank Greenberg was what *they* all said we could never be. He defied Hitler's stereotype. For that very reason, I think he may have been the single most important Jew to live in the 1930s."

—Alan Dershowitz[1]

"**I guess they** just didn't want him to beat Babe Ruth's record because of the fact that he was a Jew."[2]

That's what Detroit Tigers shortstop Billy Rogell told reporters at the end of the 1938 season, after his teammate Hank Greenberg, the team's twenty-seven-year-old first baseman, came within a couple of long foul balls of breaking the most hallowed mark in the baseball universe: Babe Ruth's 60 home runs, set in 1927 as a member of the New York Yankees. To appreciate that lofty number, consider it was more than the entire roster of any individual team in the American League that season, where the average was 55.

It was Ruth who earned credit for revolutionizing the game. Before he arrived on the scene as a nineteen-year-old pitcher for the Boston Red Sox, baseball was played in a "scientific method," with practitioners such as Ty Cobb, Napoleon Lajoie, Eddie Collins, and "Shoeless" Joe Jackson who slashed line drives, dropped down bunts for base hits, and stole bases. Brute strength like the kind displayed by Ruth and his ilk was looked down on. The home runs that went over the outfield wall were considered an aberration. (In his memoir *My Life In Baseball: The True Record*, Cobb wrote that the surge in home runs heralded by Ruth and company "have brought on a degeneration of the batting art . . ."[3])

The Sultan of Swat brought a new excitement during the Roaring Twenties, when things became bigger, brighter, and louder. Having just come out of World War I, young people were anxious to party hearty, and Ruth was the poster boy for the good-time Charlies.

The Depression was winding down after a decade. Ten years of suffering—financially, physically, mentally, emotionally, and spiritually—had taken their toll. Families displaced, men and women thrown out of work, children hungry. President Franklin Delano Roosevelt had introduced the New Deal, a series of unprecedented government programs designed to help the country get back on its feet, giving people jobs and building up American infrastructure with highways, parks, and construction projects. But it was a long, slow process.

Baseball tried to do its part as well, offering heroes like Ruth and his teammate Lou Gehrig—a couple of boys who overcame impoverished childhoods to become highly-paid stars: Ruth lived the life of wine, women, and song while Gehrig was the strong silent type (not to mention a bit of a mama's boy). The members of the press saw it as their responsibility to build up the athletes and their heroic deeds, sometimes embellishing their ordinary stories with tales of hardship to make their success all the more compelling.

With so much happening on the domestic front, Americans could be forgiven for not paying close attention to the turmoil spreading over Europe. The situation in Germany and its neighbors became increasingly unstable almost on a daily basis. The Nazis passed the Nuremberg Laws in 1935, severely curtailing the rights of Germany's Jewish citizenry. They were barred from certain professions and schools, forbidden to own firearms or intermarry with Aryan Germans, and deprived of other civil liberties. There was no place in the country for the people of Abraham, no matter that they had been living and contributing to that nation's history and culture for centuries. They were basically faced with two difficult choices: leave, usually with little more than a suitcase and the clothes on their backs (if they were that lucky), or die.

But where would they go? Many countries, including the United States, instituted a system of quotas limiting the number of émigrés, although in many cases it was really the Jews they were trying to keep out. One of the most heartbreaking examples was the trek to nowhere of the SS *St. Louis* in 1939.

The ship, with its manifest of more than 900 Jewish passengers, left Hamburg to cross the Atlantic bound for Cuba. From there, these refugees were hoping to travel on to the United States. Upon arrival at their destination, the ship encountered a bureaucratic nightmare that ultimately resulted—after another month on the water—in a return voyage to Europe. Fortunately, four countries—Belgium, France, Holland, and the United Kingdom—agreed to provide temporary refuge thanks in part to the financial backing of the American Jewish Joint Distribution Committee, which posted a cash guarantee of $500,000 (more than $8 million in 2016 dollars) to defray costs. Unfortunately, the story does not have a happy ending: more than 250 of those passengers, forced to return to their homeland, died during the Holocaust.

The European refugee crisis worsened over the course of the year. Germany annexed Austria before the baseball season started and moved into Czechoslovakia before it ended. Headlines became increasingly dire over the summer and continued into the fall. Many Americans became concerned about possible additional economic drains if the displaced were allowed to settle on US soil.

Politicians and observers in Europe tried to downplay the severity of the situation, unable or unwilling to believe anecdotal reports coming out of the regions. Numbers varied widely about the number of people imperiled. Was it 150,000? Was it 180,000? Was it more? Who was doing the counting and how accurate was it?

European neighbors who were still free of the Nazi stranglehold closed their borders. Jews were rounded up and sent off to prison, work camps, or concentration camps.

Some nations were sympathetic to the Jews' plight, but either did not change their immigration policies or made it even more difficult. As Michael R. Marrus wrote in *The Unwanted: European Refugees in the Twentieth Century*, "The stress of refugees was now becoming a giant rushing current."[4]

Roosevelt called for an international conference on refugees that was held in France in early July. As expected, it was mostly just lip service, with little in the way of actual policy-making. "One delegate after another read statements into the record, justifying existing restrictive policies and congratulating themselves on how much had already been accomplished for refugees. . . . To the consternation of Jewish representatives in mid-1938, [the conference] simply underscored the unwillingness of the western countries to receive Jewish refugees."[5]

At least the Greenberg family didn't have that to worry about. The search for the "American Dream" had brought Hank's parents, David and Sarah, from Romania at the turn of the century. They met at a social gathering for Romanians on the Lower East Side of Manhattan, fell in love, married, and set up a household where their children, Ben, Lillian, Hank (whom they intended to name Hyman but a clerical mistake Anglicized it to Henry), and Joe were born.

David Greenberg earned a good enough living and made some smart investments that allowed him to move his brood from Greenwich Village, which was not yet an uber-hip neighborhood, to a relatively upscale section of the Bronx.

Like many immigrant parents, the Greenbergs wanted their children to study hard so they could have solid professions. In their minds, academics were the key to success. Unfortunately they thought "Hymie" wasted too much time at nearby Crotona Park playing basketball, baseball, and soccer. While Ben became a lawyer and Lillian a teacher, Mama and Papa Greenberg were initially bemused by Hank's avocation (and later vocation). He often kidded that his parents raised two accomplished kids and a bum. (The youngest of the four, Joe, tried his hand as a professional ballplayer like his older brother but never made it to the major leagues.)

Hank was successful enough on the various playing fields and courts to earn an athletic scholarship to New York University, but he was more an athlete-athlete than a student-athlete. His parents eventually came around and enjoyed having a celebrity for a son.

His talents attracted the attention of baseball scouts, including Paul Krichell, who had signed Lou Gehrig. Krichell attended one of Greenberg's high school games, originally intending to look at some pitcher whose name is lost to time. Instead, he approached Greenberg, asking if he had any desire to play professional ball.

"I told him I was interested," Greenberg said in a 1938 interview with J.G. Taylor Spink, publisher of *The Sporting News*. "But after I took a few looks at Henry Louis Gehrig, I said to myself: 'Hank, here is one player who will go on and on, and there is no sense in your tying up with the Yankees and trying to wait for Gehrig to wear out. You will spend your days in the minors.'"[6] Turns out Greenberg made the right call. (He began his professional career in 1930, when Gehrig was in his eighth of seventeen seasons with the Yankees.)

The New York Giants actually had the first crack at Greenberg, as they were the team of choice around the house. After he had graduated from James Monroe High School in the Bronx, his father arranged an appointment with manager John McGraw.

But after waiting for two hours, father and son had had enough. That was when they decided Hank would take his talents elsewhere. Years later, McGraw, a Hall of Fame manager who won ten pennants and three world championships with the Giants over thirty-three seasons, would dismissively recount the missed opportunity: "Greenberg? Greenberg? Oh, I remember him. He was too awkward."[7]

Greenberg eventually signed with the Detroit Tigers in 1929. He spent three seasons in the minors playing in places like Beaumont, Texas; Raleigh, North Carolina; and Evansville, Indiana, where he encountered a degree of anti-Semitism that was much more pronounced than it was on the streets of New York.

Then again, it was a curious choice that Greenberg chose to spend half the year in perhaps the most anti-Semitic major metropolitan area in the country. In the first place, it was Henry Ford's city. Not only were his motor companies the biggest employer in the state, but he was also publisher of the *Dearborn Independent*, an anti-Jewish screed that once ran an article blaming Jews for the "Black Sox" scandal of 1919 in which the highly favored Chicago White Sox lost the World Series to the underdog Cincinnati Reds. Eight Sox players were indicted—though none were actually convicted by a court of law—and eventually banned for life by the newly installed Commissioner Kennesaw Mountain Landis. Writing for the *Independent*, W.J. Cameron blamed the fiasco on Arnold Rothstein, the mastermind behind the affair. "If fans wish to know the trouble with American baseball, they have it in three words: too much Jew."[8]

Then there was Father Charles Coughlin, a Canadian-born Roman Catholic priest, who could also be considered the de facto inventor of the archconservative, hate-spewing talk-radio format. Like Ford, he blamed many of the woes plaguing the nation—including the Depression and President Roosevelt's "Jew Deal"—on that religion.

The Motor City had the fourth largest population in the US at the time, with 1.5 million residents by the early 1930s. Many had moved there because factory work had been so available. As the United States sank further into the economic abyss, Detroit suffered more than most other metropolitan areas as its main source of income decreased from five million in 1929 to three million the following year to 1.3 million the next. Dark times opened the door for desperation as people looked for both answers and a place to lay blame. Organizations such as the Ku Klux Klan and the Black Legion gained in misguided popularity. Thankfully, Hank Greenberg managed to remain unscathed by that violent situation, at least physically.

Notes

1. *Hero of Heroes*, p. 163.
2. Ibid, p. 171.
3. Ty Cobb and Al Stump, *My Life in Baseball: The True Record* (Bison Books, 1993), p. 145.
4. **Michael R. Marrus, *The Unwanted: European Refugees in the Twentieth Century* (Oxford University Press, 1985).**
5. Ibid, pp. 171–72.
6. J. G. Taylor Spink, "Hitting the High Spots with Hank Greenberg." *The Sporting News*, January 20, 1938.
7. Arnold C. Burr, "Bargains in Future stars Frequently Muffed by Officials." *The Sporting News*, January 5, 1938.
8. W. J. Cameron, "Jewish Degradation of American Baseball." *Dearborn Independent*, September 10, 1921.

SPRING TRAINING

"I am nobody's dummy."—Hank Greenberg telling the press he would no longer take signs about incoming pitches from coach Del Baker.[1]

When spring training opened for the upcoming 1938 season, the Detroit Tigers were three years removed from their first—and to that point only—world's championship. They had won three straight American League pennants between 1907 and 1909, but lost each fall classic—two to the Chicago Cubs and the third to the Pittsburgh Pirates. They would wait another twenty-five years for their next first-place finish, but once again came up short in the World Series, this time to the St. Louis Cardinals' "Gashouse Gang."

In 1935, the Tigers rode their young slugger Hammerin' Hank Greenberg into the postseason. He won the major league RBI crown with 168—38 more than his closest competitor, Wally Berger of the NL's Boston Braves—and tied the Philadelphia A's strongman Jimmie Foxx for the major league lead in home runs with 36. Greenberg also led the junior circuit (a nickname for the American

League) with 389 total bases and finished in the top ten in several other categories including runs scored (third with 120), hits (fourth with 203), batting average (seventh with a .328 mark), slugging (second at .628), on-base percentage (sixth at .411), doubles (second with 46), walks (sixth with 87), and at-bats per home run (second at 17.2). He even finished third with 16 triples; not bad for a guy John McGraw refused to even consider for a tryout because he was too awkward and slow.

The six-foot, three-inch first sacker was no slouch with a mitt either. Surprisingly agile for a big man, he finished either first or second in the league in games, putouts, assists, and double plays in 1935. All this made him the logical—and unanimous—selection for American League MVP. Greenberg's World Series against the Cubs, however, was a bust—literally.

After going hitless in the opener, Greenberg blasted a two-run homer off Charlie Root in the second game, part of a four-run inning for the Tigers en route to an 8–3 win. In the seventh inning, with one out and Charlie Gehringer on first, Greenberg was hit on the left wrist by a pitch from Fabian Kowalik. He flexed his arm a little on the way to first but, with the pride of the athlete, refused to let on how much it really hurt.

Goose Goslin followed Greenberg and flied out to left for the second out, bringing Pete Fox to the plate. The right fielder singled to his Cubs counterpart, driving in Gehringer. With two outs, Greenberg was off and running. He galloped (although perhaps lumbered is a better description) around the bases, hesitating for just a split second at third before continuing on his ill-advised journey. He crashed into Gabby Hartnett, the Cubs' six-foot-one, 195-pound catcher, who landed heavily on Greenberg's already injured wrist, holding on to the ball for the third out.

Greenberg walked to the dugout cradling his arm. In his mind, he must have known that something was seriously wrong, but in his heart he was unwilling to admit a worst-case scenario. Despite immediate post-game treatments and more the next day, the pain proved to be too much and the Tigers' best man was done for the remainder of the Series.

As it happened, the sixth and final game—a 4–3 win for the Tigers—fell on October 7: Yom Kippur, the holiest day on the Jewish calendar. Just the year before, Greenberg had become a national figure by acceding to the wishes of his family and the tenets of his religion by refusing to play in a crucial game even though it came right in the midst of a pennant race. For some reason, though, he decided the 1935 World Series was an entirely different kettle of gefilte fish and indicated he *would* play this time around. Had he done so, it might have changed the way some— especially his Jewish fans—thought about him, negating the good will from the previous year. The injury made that all a moot point, taking the decision out of his hands. Perhaps larger forces were at play. Greenberg was happy for the team, of course; the Tigers had won their first World Series title. But he was disappointed he had not been able to have more of a role.

It was only after Detroit had clinched the championship that X-rays revealed Greenberg had several small cracks in his wrist.

The injury proved to be a crucial factor in the Tigers' under-achievements in 1936. In the April 29 game against the Washington Senators, Jake Powell ran into Greenberg at first base. "The accident occurred when the big first baseman, reaching to the left for a wide throw, collided with Powell, who was racing to the bag," according to an Associated Press story. "As Powell sped past, his left arm caught Greenberg's and wrenched it back. Hank fell to the ground and after a hurried examination on the field was rushed to a hospital."[2] X-rays revealed the wrist was broken again.

There was a good deal of conjecture that Powell had deliberately sought to injure the Jewish ballplayer. He had earned a reputation over the years as an unrepentant bigot, once telling reporters he kept in shape during the off-season by serving as an "honorary" police officer in Dayton, Ohio, where he "beat niggers over the head with [his] blackjack."[3]

Initially, Greenberg was only supposed to miss a month to six weeks, but in reality his season was over after just 12 games. Detroit finished in second place with a 83–71 record, 19.5 games behind the Yankees who ran away with the pennant, winning 102 before beating the Giants in the World Series.

Greenberg returned to robust health for the 1937 campaign, bashing 40 home runs and driving in a major league–best 184 runs—third highest in the history of the game behind Hack Wilson's 191 and Lou Gehrig's 185—but the team's results were the same: second place, albeit with a slightly better mark of 89–65, 13 games behind the Yankees, who repeated as World Series champs, again over their cross-river rival.

With most of the starting position players returning for 1938, hopes were high as the Tigers prepared for the new season and looked to improve on the previous year. While they fell short of the AL title, finishing 13 games behind the Yankees, they still had an impressive 89 wins. And while it was the most wins they'd had since their title year of '35, what was most impressive was the success they had with their bats, leading the AL in hits, batting average, and on-base percentage, and coming in second in home runs, RBIs, runs, doubles, stolen bases, slugging average, and total bases.

The double play combo, one of the best in the game, was intact heading into '38 with Greenberg at first, Charlie Gehringer (a.k.a. "The Mechanical Man" for his steady play) at second, and switch-hitting Billy Rogell at short. Third base would be entrusted to Don Ross, a twenty-three-year-old rookie, while Rudy York, a promising slugger without a real defensive position, was once again behind the plate, at least for the time being.

Prior to the new season, it was York whom sports prognosticators chose as a possible new home run king. In its issue of April 7, *The Sporting News* declared, "York, Who Fought Four Years for Tiger Job, Seeks New 'Break'—Ruth's 60-Homer Record" while *Newsweek* thought enough of that possibility to put him on the cover of their April 18 edition positing the question, "Rudy York—Greatest Slugger Since Babe Ruth?"

Pete Fox was set to anchor right field following his 12 home runs and 82 RBIs in 1937. Chet Morgan, who had made his big league debut with the Tigers in 1935 before returning to the minors for the next two seasons, was back to play center. Dixie Walker, acquired from the Chicago White Sox in a six-player deal in December to replace Gee Walker (no relation), was handed the responsibility of patrolling left.

In the years before September call-ups allowed teams to have up to 40 on their roster (not to mention the inordinate number of replacements for those on the disabled list), the Tigers used just 31 players for the entire 1937 season, including only 13 pitchers. (Compare that with the 2016 Tigers, who used 44 players, 22 of them pitchers.)

The starting rotation completed the league average of 70 games in 1937. Vern Kennedy, at thirty-one, was the ace of the staff, having been acquired during the offseason in the Walker deal. He was followed by George Gill, the submarine-throwing Elden Auker, Tommy Bridges, Roxie Lawson, and the brilliantly nicknamed Boots Poffenberger. Boots, at twenty-two years of age, was the baby of the group.

Cochrane counted on Harry Eisenstat, a former Dodger, and Slick Coffman, in his sophomore season, to be the mainstays out of the bullpen. They would be backed up by Al Benton and Jake Wade. Like Greenberg, Eisenstat had grown up in an observant Jewish household in New York City.[4]

Beginning in 1934, and with the exception of 1943–45 when travel restrictions required teams to prepare for the season closer to their home cities (in their case, Evansville, Indiana), the Tigers spent spring training in Lakeland, Florida. The home ballpark, Henley Field, was named for a local drug store merchant (but was rebranded Joker Marchant Stadium in 1967). Located just 35 miles east of Tampa, Lakeland's warm, sunny climate has historically been conducive for the citrus business that still accounts for a sizeable portion of the local economy. The industry suffered a setback during the Depression, as did a substantial portion of the country. But instead of dust storms, it was an infestation of Mediterranean fruit flies that cut production by more than half in the late twenties.

The Tigers arrived for spring training confident in their abilities. Who knows how far they could go with a fully recovered Hank Greenberg? Maybe "Hankus Pankus" (a nickname bestowed upon him by Ty Tyson, a popular Detroit radio broad-caster) would get a break and go through the forthcoming season without major injury, suggested Bill McGowan, an American League umpire and writer, in *The Sporting News.* "If he does, watch for some records to fall."[5] McGowan was not so bold as to predict which records those might be, however.

Greenberg was also feeling his oats, looking for a bigger sal-ary and declaring he was his own man at the plate. Sure, he had taken some signs from his coach Del Baker, who had an uncanny ability to pick up the opposing catcher's signs and relay to the hitters what pitch might be coming, but that was over. In a Q&A format interview with J.G. Taylor Spink, publisher of *The Sporting News*, Greenberg said, "The word has spread around that if I do not get the sign, I can't hit. That is not so. . . . I believe the time has come for Hank Greenberg to get out on his own, and get the credits, or the blame, on his own."[6]

"I've got a hunch the Yankees are going to blow up in a large way this year," Greenberg told reporters in January. He would have done better to keep such predictions to himself: Not only did the Bombers end up winning their straight World Championship, but his other forecasts—that the Giants would "win it in a walk" and that Dizzy Dean would win 25 games—were similarly mis-guided. The Giants finished third in the NL and Dean, after several years as the ace of the Cardinals staff, appeared in just 13 games for his *new* team, the Chicago Cubs. The Dean deal was the biggest news during spring training. The Cubs acquired him from their perennial archrivals right before the trading deadline in exchange for three players and $185,000, the second highest monetary figure to date after the $250,000 the Boston Red Sox paid for future Hall of Famer Joe Cronin.

By all accounts, the Tigers enjoyed a successful spring tune-up, winning 18 of 27 games. Greenberg presaged the reliable contributor he would be during the regular season by leading his team in most offensive categories, including at-bats, runs, hits, home runs, and runs batted in; he and York combined for 16 of the team's 26 round-trippers with nine and seven, respectively. In the final game at Lakeland before heading north, Greenberg hit a mammoth shot in a 7–6 win over the Montreal Royals of the International League. Despite the great distance, it was, amazingly, not a home run but a very long out. The Montreal outfielder "went half way to Winter Haven to haul down the long fly ball," wrote Charles Ward in the *Free Press* account.

"The ball must have travelled 500 feet," according to Ward. "It was hit so hard that Roy Cullenbine was able to score from second base after the catch." One of Greenberg's teammates joked that the outfielder had to have been playing "out of bounds" to make the play.[7]

In a brief preseason assessment for *The Sporting News*, Bill Dooly, who normally plied his trade for the *Philadelphia Record*, determined that the new batch of Tigers were "a pretty fair country ball club, say we, one that might very well win the American League burgee" (burgee being just a five-dollar word for the pennant).[8]

But all this was just the usual optimistic build-up, with many teams working out their personnel and experimenting with one thing or another. Once the campaign began, each organization would start out on an equal footing in the standings. It would be different once the bell rang on Opening Day. The time had come to see what the real season had in store.

The optimism that surrounded the return of baseball after a long cold winter could not, however, keep real world issues from continuing to cast a pall on more significant matters, at least according to fans.

In March, Adolf Hitler and his Nazi followers made their first major move in their quest for global domination with the *Anschluss*—the annexation of Austria—ostensibly to protect the rights of residents of German heritage. Well, not *all* Austrians of German heritage. That is, not the Jews. A series of increasingly restrictive measures which began with the Nuremberg Laws were put in place to make that population as miserable as possible, including the registration of any property owned by Jews valued at over 5,000 Reichmarks ($21,000 in 1938 dollars, almost $345,000 in 2016).

> In the Jewish quarter of Vienna boys were flogged, the eyes of old men watered as their beards were jerked. Nazis spat in the face of Jewesses, and almost everyone whether Jew or Aryan was soon wearing a swastika. Later Jews were forbidden to wear them.[9]

It is well beyond the scope of this book to examine the causes and events of domestic and international politics during that timeframe, but some facts are elementary: the Nazis blamed the Jews for the majority of their problems (and the world's ills) and wanted them removed from German society. At first it seemed they might be content with just driving the Jews out of the country, forcing them to uproot after centuries of residence despite their incalculable contributions in the fields of art, music, literature, science, and more. Soon—but at the same time too slowly—it became evident that Germany found the mere existence of the Jewish race anathema. The Jews were a disease and the problems would only continue if the "virus" was not eradicated.

The situation proved unbearable for some Jews who had neither the financial means nor opportunity to relocate to better circumstances. The Jewish Telegraphic Agency, considered the wire service for the Jewish news world, reported that with Austria clamping down on measures to prevent its Jewish residents from leaving the country, some 1,700 people—"most of them professionals, merchants and scientists"—had chosen to commit suicide rather than live under Nazi rule.

"While Jews continued to besiege consulates for visas, it was apparent that the authorities here were under orders to make Jewish emigration practically impossible," the JTA recounted under a Vienna dateline in late March.[10]

Such news did little to melt the hearts of American isolationists, as well as European nations outside German sway, who combined the fear and hatred of the foreign with continued anxiety over economic instability. An editorial in the May 1938 *Defender* magazine was typical of the sentiment: "Let us stop immigration completely for a while and give our present alien population an opportunity to become Americanized before they foreignize us." Only slightly more charitable was a piece in *The New York Times* that conceded "Even the United States, with its immense area and resources, cannot be expected to perform today, with millions of its own people unemployed, the historic service it has previously performed in giving unlimited refuge to the victims of political and religious persecution."[11] President Roosevelt's own cousin, Laura

Delano Houghteling, wife of the US commissioner of immigration, warned "20,000 charming children would all too soon grow into 20,000 ugly adults."[12]

As the simmering threats in Europe began to reach their boiling point, small news items no more than three or four paragraphs slowly migrated from deep within the tabloids and broadsheets to larger headlines and front page articles. They had little positive effect. A poll by *Fortune* magazine published in July 1938 asked, "What is your attitude toward allowing German, Austrian, and other political refugees to come into the United States?" Although the publication has traditionally been geared toward a more well-to-do and better-educated readership, there is no indication to whom the question was posed. Nevertheless, less than five percent agreed with the proffered response: "We should encourage them to come even if we have to raise our immigration quotas." An overwhelming majority—67.4 percent—aligned with the answer: "With conditions as they are, we should try to keep them out." Nor were respondents more generous early the following year when the question was revised to allow only children to enter the country: in this case the results were 30 percent agreeing and 61 percent denying a change in policy.[13]

In early November 1938, the Nazis unleashed *Kristallnacht* (the Night of Broken Glass), two days of mob violence and vandalism that resulted in scores of deaths and the destruction of thousands of Jewish businesses, homes, schools, and synagogues. In addition, thirty thousand Jews were sent to concentration camps. The Nazis justified their actions by claiming these demonstrations came as a result of the assassination of a member of the German consulate stationed in France by Herschel Grynszpan, a seventeen-year-old Jew who sought revenge after members of his family had been evicted from their home and business by German police in Poland.

This marked the unofficial beginning of open season on Jews.

A poll conducted by the Gallup Organization in the US two weeks after *Kristallnacht* offered some seemingly contradictory information, although it confirmed earlier attitudes:

> Do you approve or disapprove of the Nazi's treatment . . .
> of Jews in Germany?
>> Approve: 5.6%
>> Disapprove: 88.2%
>> No Opinion: 6.2%

> Should we allow a larger number of Jewish exiles from Germany to come to the United States to live?
>> Yes: 21.2%
>> No: 71.8%
>> No Opinion: 7%

Shockingly, nearly 65 percent of the respondents said, "the prosecution of the Jews in Europe has been their own fault" either entirely or in part.[14]

Is it any wonder that Americans—even (especially?) American Jews—sought to find a few hours respite through the simple game of baseball?

Notes

1. "Greenberg Tired of Being Baker's Charley McCarthy." *Pittsburgh Post-Gazette*, January 4, 1938.

2. "Hank Greenberg Breaks Wrist in Collision; Snaps Same Arm Hurt in World Series Last Year." *Rochester Democrat and Chronicle*, April 30, 1936.

3. Steve Wulf, "Bigot unwittingly sparked change." ESPN. com, February 22, 2014

4. The 1938 season would be Eisenstat's only full season in Detroit. He was traded to the Cleveland Indians in the middle of the 1939 season, where he pitched for the remainder of his career.

5. Bill McGowan, "Big Hank All Hitched to Go to Town." *The Sporting News*, January 6, 1938.

6. J. G. Taylor Spink, "Hitting the High Spots with Hank Greenberg." *The Sporting News*, January 20, 1938.

7. Charles P. Ward, "Schoolboy Rescues Auker to Give Tigers Sixteenth Victory." *Detroit Free Press*, April 11, 1938.

8. "How They Look for 1938 . . . Detroit Tigers." *The Sporting News*, February 24, 1938.

9. "Hitler Comes Home." *Time*, March 21, 1938.

10. "'Suicidal' Wave Sweeps Austria." *Sentinel*, March 24, 1938.

11. "The Refugees." *The New York Times*, November 9, 1938.

12. "Kristallnacht and the World's Response." *The Jewish Week*, Aish.com/ho/i/48957091.html

13. Ishaan Tharoor, "What Americans thought of Jewish refugees on the eve of World War II." *Washington Post*, November 17, 2015.

14. 1938 Gallup Polls on Jews, volokh.com/posts/1226283758. shtml

APRIL

"Hank Greenberg was an honest worker in a time of trial in Detroit and his perseverance inspired our city in ways that raised the spirits of those who saw him perform."[1]

—Joe Falls

To paraphrase the theme song of the Depression, happy days were here again. At least they were for baseball-starved fans who had endured another long winter waiting for Opening Day with all the associated enthusiasm that represented the hopes for a country which had been making very slow inroads to economic recovery.

Going to a ball game was still a bit of a luxury for many fans, and teams increasingly felt that pinch over the years. The US government exacerbated the problem by adding a 10 percent tax on tickets costing more than forty cents, which, not surprisingly, had a negative impact when it came to the sale of the higher-priced ducats. A box seat in the lower deck at the newly rechristened Briggs Stadium cost $1.50, plus an additional fifteen cents in taxes.

Owners did what they could to control expenses by cutting salaries and even the size of rosters, dropping two spots from the customary 25 to 23. Major league attendance—and consequently profits—fell alarmingly, from 10.1 million in 1930 to 6.3 million in 1933. The perennially awful St. Louis Browns *averaged* just 120,000 fans over the course of the decade.

The Tigers were not immune from the suffering. In 1933, they hosted a mere 320,972 guests, their worst showing since 1918, when 203,719 patrons went through the turnstiles. Things improved significantly over the next two seasons as the team won two pennants, with attendance almost tripling to 919,161 in 1934 and going over the million mark (1,034,929) for the second time in franchise history the following season.

The minor leagues were similarly in peril. In 1929, the last season before the stock market crash, 26 leagues, comprised of 182 teams, were in operation. Even before the Depression not every team made it through to the end of the season. Some might relocate or merge with another club, but it was not unheard of for entire leagues to fold due to poor attendance or other business difficulties. As one might expect, the situation fluctuated greatly over the next dozen years.

While major league clubs often had individual arrangements by which they could send a player to a minor league team for seasoning since the nineteenth century, the formal affiliations currently in use began in the early 1930s. Branch Rickey, who later signed Jackie Robinson as the first African American to play in the majors, is credited with creating the farm system as we now know it.

According to Baseball-Reference.com, the number of minor leagues and teams dipped to a low point in 1933 but slowly rebounded by the end of the decade.

Year	Leagues	Teams	Affiliates
1930	23	158	8
1931	19	136	5
1932	19	134	42
1933	14	101	32
1934	20	136	46
1935	21	148	69
1936	26	184	107
1937	37	254	139
1938	37	261	134

It's worth noting that in the teeth of the Depression, the Tigers were in the middle among the teams in fewest farm clubs. They had agreements with five affiliates in 1932, six in 1933, four in 1934, six in 1935, nine in 1936 and 1937, and six in 1938 when the AL average was almost eight. In 1938, the Cardinals had control of 27 teams, far and away the most of any major league club; the Yankees were the closest with twelve.

In spite of all the problems threatening the country and the national pastime, baseball commissioner Kennesaw Mountain Landis tried to be optimistic. Speaking at the annual convention of the National Association of Professional Baseball Leagues in Galveston, Texas, in 1933, he said: "A man can't go to a baseball game when he hasn't any money. He won't have money as long as he doesn't have a job. The American people love baseball. Many of them now peer over the fence or through it, and they will return as paying customers as soon as they have money."[2]

While the economy had gradually improved since 1929, it suffered a downturn in 1937 as President Roosevelt, convinced that the US had turned a corner thanks to his New Deal, sought to balance the federal budget by closing some programs that were deemed no longer necessary to the country's recovery. It was a bold decision but proved to be a premature one. Unemployment jumped from 14.3 to 19 percent while manufacturing output fell by almost 40 percent, erasing much of the progress of the previous three years.

With jobs so hard to come by, ballplayers frequently hid their injuries, afraid if they took even a few days off the front office would call up someone from their farm teams to take their place. Even if modern medical technology had been available back then, it's questionable whether many would have taken advantage of it. Starting pitchers regularly tossed 250 innings or more through sore arms, bone spurs, and the like. You know there's no way Lou Gehrig went through 2,130 consecutive games unscathed; he was just lucky not to have any serious issues.

Some teams went a step further to reduce their costs, employing one person to both play *and* manage, thereby saving a roster spot (and an additional salary). That's how Mickey Cochrane wound up with the Tigers in 1934. For nine seasons, the Boston University graduate was a fierce leader for the Philadelphia A's and one of the best catchers to ever play the game. The team won three straight pennants from 1929 to 1931 and took two of the three World Series. Despite their heady accomplishments—or perhaps because of it since good teams mean higher payrolls—A's owner and manager Connie Mack was forced to sell off some of his stars in order to keep the team afloat.

Cochrane was one of those causalities of success, going to the Tigers for $100,000 a player named Johnny Pasek, whose entire big-league career consisted of 32 games over two seasons.

The Tigers picked up a real bargain, paying him $30,000 to take on both chores. Even with the additional responsibility, Cochrane performed valiantly. Not only did he lead the Tigers to their first pennant in twenty-five years, but won AL MVP honors. He was even better in 1935, piloting the team to its first world's championship. He even scored the winning run in the bottom of the ninth in the final game to beat the Chicago Cubs. Preston Sturges couldn't have scripted it better.

Cochrane, who was inducted into the Hall of Fame in 1947, had a reputation as being somewhat "high-strung," and the dual responsibilities eventually took their toll. He suffered a nervous breakdown in 1936, was hospitalized for a while, and spent additional time recuperating as the Tigers dropped to second place. The following year, on May 25 against the New York Yankees, Cochrane was beaned by a pitch from Bump Hadley, resulting in a near-fatal triple skull fracture. Though he recovered and resumed his managerial duties, he would never play another official major league game.

Some 18,000 fans lucky enough to come up with the scratch visited Comiskey Park to see the White Sox host the Tigers on Opening Day, April 19, 1938. They were part of 192,000 throughout baseball rolling through the turnstiles to break the winter doldrums and inaugurate a new season. The blustery

Chicago weather had improved markedly from the beginning of the month when snow was still falling. Now, and through the end of April, the Windy City would enjoy higher than average temperatures—ones more suitable for July.

For Chicago, the assignment of Opening Day starter fell to John Whitehead, a twenty-nine-year-old righty who won 37 games over his first three seasons but was now on the downside of his career. "Silent John" retired the first two batters before giving up a single to Gehringer. Greenberg followed with a walk in his first plate appearance of the new season. Whitehead stemmed any damage by retiring York on a foul ball to the catcher.

Prior to the new season, it was York whom a number of "experts" picked as the new power run king . . . but it was Greenberg who was first on the board. Trailing 4–1 with two outs in the fifth inning, he launched a solo shot into the left field stands for home run number one. The Tigers tacked on a run in the ninth on a pinch-hit round-tripper by Chet Laabs, but the Sox held on for the 4–3 win, giving their admirers an extra degree of warmth. The whole affair in the pre-television days was concluded in a tidy one hour and fifty-nine minutes.

The Tigers found themselves on the wrong side of a one-run decision again the next day as the White Sox eked out a 5–4 win in front of just 3,500 game-goers, a far cry from the number of hardy souls on hand for the opener.

Greenberg was hitless in three official at bats although he did reach base twice on walks. He made the final out in the first, third, and fifth innings, each time leaving men on base, anathema for a man who prided himself on driving in runs.

The Tigers finally got untracked, winning the third game of the series in Chicago in dominating style, 9–3. In the sixth inning, Greenberg blasted another solo job, becoming only the second batter to put one over the roof of Comiskey's left field pavilion; rival slugger Jimmie Foxx had accomplished the feat two years earlier.

Greenberg's second home run in three games temporarily gave his team a 3–2 lead. Preseason scouting reports of the White Sox's porous defense turned out to be accurate as catcher Tony Rensa made one error and first baseman Joe Kuhel committed a pair to go along with some shaky performances by four Chicago hurlers who combined to issue nine walks. Greenberg received two of those freebies, including an intentional pass in the seventh to load the bases. It proved a smart move for the moment, but Detroit still put up a four-spot. He completed his game with, of all things, a bunt single in the ninth.

Greenberg's prowess at the plate was becoming the stuff of song and story, comparable to tales of medieval knights. Although this little ditty wasn't composed until Greenberg had joined the Pittsburgh Pirates more than a decade later, the lyrics aptly described his entire career:

> Goodbye, Mr. Ball, goodbye.
> You are going to see an awful lot of sky.
> Don't hang around for Richard to open up that door
> when Hankus Pankus hits you where you've never been hit before . . . [3]

The front-page headlines of the *Detroit Free Press* on Friday, April 22 ranged from the important . . .

"Peace Talks Called as U.A.W. Walkout Shuts Bohn Plants"
"Roosevelt Will Ask Ford for Plan to Stabilize Work in Auto Plants"
"Lindbergh-Carrel Machine Develops Human Embryo"

to the ridiculous . . .

"Forced to Live at 105"
"Two Nude Models Seized Posing for Camera Fans"
"Roosevelt Going Fishing if Congress Will Let Him."

But there was nothing about what was really on the minds of baseball fans: The return of baseball to Motown.

Although the temperatures were a bit on the cool side, settling in the mid-fifties, it was nonetheless a picture perfect day for the Tigers to kick off the new season at Briggs Stadium, rechristened for owner Walter Briggs who oversaw the expansion of the stadium's capacity from 36,000 to 53,000 following the death of former owner Frank Navin, for whom the field had been named in 1912.

The Tigers led the American League in attendance in 1937 and they were off in good fashion as more than 54,000 packed the landmark ball yard at the intersection of Michigan and Trumbull, Detroit's answer—at least on this day—to Hollywood and Vine or Broadway and 42nd as the crossroads of their baseball world. The J. L. Hudson Department store took out an advertisement in the *Detroit Free Press*, wishing the team well and in particular welcoming the newcomers to the Tigers' staff: "You'll find Detroit fans consistently to be good sports."

The three o'clock game was preceded by a parade up Lafayette Boulevard, highlighted by a caravan of 18 Tigers old-timers. While the only names modern hard-core fans might recognize would be Davy Jones, Bobby Veach, and Eddie Cicotte, the *Free Press* characterized the group as "a pretty good ball club if you ask your old dad."[4] (Cicotte played just three games for the Tigers in his debut season in 1905. He was known more infamously as a member of the White Sox who were expelled from baseball for allegedly throwing games in the 1919 "Black Sox" scandal. I use the word "allegedly" because Cicotte and the other seven co-conspirators were never convicted in a court of law.)

After Detroit Mayor Richard W. Reading tossed out the ceremonial first pitch in shirtsleeves and vest, the record-setting crowd was treated to a tight, tense ball game. It was a pity they had to leave disappointed when the visiting Cleveland Indians took the 4–3 decision behind the complete-game efforts of Mel Harder. Greenberg's only contribution at the plate was an opposite field triple to right to lead off the fourth.

Trailing by a run, Cochrane employed some puzzling strategy when he allowed Schoolboy Rowe—who came on in relief of starter Tommy Bridges and pitched the final five frames—to lead off for the Tigers in the bottom of the ninth. Rowe had a lifetime batting average of .263 with 18 home runs, so perhaps his manager was playing a hunch. Unfortunately, it did not pay off and the Tigers went down in order to give the Indians their third straight win, heralded on the front page of the *Cleveland Plain Dealer* along with a photo of the young movie star Shirley Temple, who was celebrating her ninth birthday. Temple rivaled the greatest sports heroes in terms of popularity, putting smiles on millions of faces through her singing and dancing in films such as *Little Miss Broadway* and *Rebecca of Sunnybrook Farm*, both of which premiered in 1938.

Greenberg and his fans would have to suffer through two more losses to the Indians before he launched his next home run—another solo pop—against Ed Cole of the host St. Louis Browns in a 10–1 win on April 25. He would undoubtedly have agreed with T.S. Eliot: April *was* the cruelest month, the worst for him over his career. His "slash line" (batting average, on-base percentage, and slugging percentage) was a mortal-like .284/.407/.510 with just 16 home runs. To be fair, though, the schedule prior to 1961 consisted of 154 games, so the season normally opened later than it does nowadays. Greenberg accumulated his statistics in just 116 April games, 105 fewer than May. The first month of the 1938 campaign was par for the course with at batting average of just .231, a .400 on-base percentage, and a .538 slugging percentage. And while he did put those three balls over the wall, he had just four RBIs, falling woefully short in that department which no doubt contributed to the team's sluggish 5–6 start. By contrast, York drove in six runs in April; Billy Rogell, seven; Charlie Gehringer and Chet Laabs, eight apiece; and Dixie Walker, one ahead of Greenberg with five. Still, with so much baseball left to play, few were willing to hit the panic button just yet.

Greenberg in April:

G	PA	AB	R	H	2B	3B	HR	RBI	BB	SO	BA	OBP	SLG
11	50	39	9	9	1	1	3	4	11	9	.231	.400	.538

Notes

1 *Detroit News*, September 5, 1986.

2 "Landis Blames Baseball Slump on Depression Alone." *Altoona Tribune*, November 14, 1933.

3 The tune, written by Bill Coryn and Harold Smith, was performed by Groucho Marx, Bing Crosby—a part owner of the team—and Greenberg himself on the *Philco Radio Show* in 1947.

4 "Weatherman Promises Perfect Baseball Day." *Detroit Free Press*, April 22, 1938.

MAY

_____

"There was nobody in all of baseball who took more abuse than Hank, except Jackie Robinson."

—Birdie Tebbetts

The new month started out on the same note as the old one, with a pair of losses. The Indians were the antagonists once again, taking the first game, 4–3, on May 1 at the cavernous Municipal Stadium and 11–3 the following day at cozier League Park. (The Indians were the only team in the majors to have two home fields.) Cleveland reliever Al Milnar fanned Greenberg for the final out of the May 1 affair. Milnar had proven himself up to the challenge in his first appearance of the season, facing Dixie Walker, Charlie Gehringer, and Greenberg—the two, three, and four batters—after starter Mel Harder had given up a pinch-hit double to Jo-Jo White and a RBI single to Pete Fox, his fifth hit of the game, to move the Tigers within a run.

The high-strung Milnar, who went by the nickname "Happy," came back from a 3-0 count to induce Walker to fly out to right.

Gehringer followed with a similar play to left before Greenberg swung at and missed a 2-2 fastball across the letters.

"As Milnar dashed from the box toward the runway leading to the clubhouse, he was overwhelmed by a dozen teammates, pounding his back, wringing his hand, and shouting congratulations in his ear," wrote *Cleveland Plain Dealer* beat writer Gordon Cobbledick.[1]

The twenty-four-year-old Milnar was a local product, a fact proudly proclaimed by the press, including the *Plain Dealer*'s James E. Doyle in his column "The Sports Trail" the following day. In a fictitious conversation between two immigrant fans presented in a pidgin-English dialect that today would be considered politically incorrect, Doyle wrote, "You're should see [Milnar] strike for last h'out beeg Hank Greenberg, what's heet so motch home runs. Wuss take nerfe, I'm tell you, what dees kid wuss do."[2]

In a disastrous Monday meeting the Indians scored ten runs in the fourth inning against three Tiger hurlers at their weekday-lodgings at League Park. Harry Eisenstat took the brunt of it. He entered the game with no outs, runners on first and second, and two runs already in thanks to starter Jake Wade. After retiring the first batter he faced on a ground out, Eisenstat allowed Wade's runs to come home and then gave up five of his own on four hits and a walk before Cochrane gave him the hook.

Greenberg singled in three at-bats and also a worked out a walk, but it was what someone did to him that received even more attention in the Cleveland papers than the Indians output.

The game was already out of reach when Greenberg stepped into the batter's box in the eighth with two out, two runs in, and a runner on first. He crushed a pitch to deep center field. Roy

Weatherly, a defensive replacement for Earl Averill, took off in pursuit.

"When the ball left the bat, Roy turned his back, put down his head, and ran as only he can run for the remotest corner of the park," reported Cobbledick in the *Plain Dealer*. "[H]e left his feet in a headlong dive and got his hands on the ball just as he landed face downward in the dirt.

"Greenberg, nearly to third base, stopped and looked into the Tiger dugout for confirmation of his own eyesight. Even then he looked as if he wanted to protest to [Commissioner] Landis. And then he slouched across to his first base station, glaring at Weatherly with every step."

The ball had travelled some 450 feet. "It was a catch. . . that will go down in the books as one of the most spectacular outfield plays in the history of baseball in Cleveland," wrote Cobbledick.[3] Of course, no audio or video is available to confirm such a dramatic narrative. Hyperbole being a standard literary device in the days before television and video replay, we'll have to take his word for it.

For the series, Greenberg totaled three hits—including his second double of the season—in eleven at-bats with no RBIs, keeping him stuck at four over his first thirteen games. These days, sports websites update a player's season projections following each contest. If such analytics had been available in 1938, they would have penciled Greenberg in for just 48 ribbies, a *shande* (Yiddish for shame) for a man whose stated self-worth on the diamond was based on his ability to drive his teammates across the plate. Granted it was still fairly early in the season, but it doesn't take much to send tongues wagging when a team finds itself underachieving. The Tigers were 5–8, five games back of the first-place Indians who had won 10 of their first 13 games.

The more shocking baseball news of the day concerned Lou Gehrig. The Iron Horse had appeared in the fourth spot in the bating order in 71 percent of his 2,164 games. But the Yankees dropped him from that place of honor to number six. Joe DiMaggio, entering his third full season, took the cleanup role and homered in a 3–2 win over the Washington Senators.

It was no secret that something was ailing Gehrig. Sure, at thirty-five he was no spring chicken, definitely in the twilight of his career. But 1937 had been a most productive year: 37 home runs, 158 RBIs, 138 runs, a batting average of .351, and an OPS of 1.116, all in the top seven in the American League. However, the beginning of the 1938 spring training saw him struggling more than one might expect to get into shape, muffing plays in the field, not getting around on pitches. Of course, we now know he was in the early stages of amyotrophic lateral sclerosis, ALS, which would one day bear the name Lou Gehrig's Disease.

On May 3, Adolf Hitler embarked on a weeklong trip to Italy where he was feted by Prime Minister Benito Mussolini. Pope Pius XI, however, was not as welcoming. He lamented that the swastika—the Nazi cross—was being widely displayed in Hitler's honor in the Holy City. Mussolini warned the pope to keep his opinions to himself. "It is very dangerous to speak of and wave the cross of Christ as if it were a weapon," the Associated Press quoted Mussolini as saying.[4]

The same day Hitler arrived in Italy, the Flossenbürg concentration camp, located in Bavaria near the Czechoslovakia border, took in its first prisoner. As an example of how badly informed America was on such matters, the initial report regarding Flossenbürg did not appear in *The New York Times* for almost seven years—when the camps were liberated.

From Cleveland, the Tigers traveled to Boston's famed Fenway Park to take on the Red Sox and Jimmie Foxx, Greenberg's main-power-hitting rival at the time.

Foxx, a.k.a. "Double-X," a.k.a. "The Beast," a powerfully-built six-foot 190-pound outfielder from Sudlersville, Maryland, came close to Babe Ruth's mark in 1932, blasting 58 home runs as a member of Connie Mack's Philadelphia Athletics. Foxx won the American League MVP that season and the next as the "Mackmen" were slowly coming down to earth after winning three straight pennants from 1929 to 1931. Foxx also won the award in 1933 and 1938, making him one of only a handful of players to attain the honor three or more times.[5] Sadly, Mack felt compelled by financial reasons to send Foxx and Johnny Marcum to the Red Sox after the 1935 season for Gordon Rhodes, George Savino, and $150,000.

The Tigers continued their struggles, losing 4–3 to thirty-eight-year-old Lefty Grove in 10 innings on May 3.

Grove—like Foxx a future Hall of Famer—reached a milestone by striking out opposing pitcher Roxie Lawson for his 2,000th victim. Only eight pitchers had heretofore reached that landmark.[6]

Greenberg finally hit his fourth home run of the year, a solo shot in the second inning to tie the game at 1–1. It was his only hit in three at-bats, although he also walked twice. The loss dropped the Tigers into seventh place in the eight-team league, their lowest point in the standings all year.

They broke their three-game losing streak on May 4 with a 4–1 win. Greenberg contributed two doubles and a single, scored one run, and drove in another. The next day, he hit his second homer in three games to assist in a 7–5 victory. Perhaps more entertaining to the 5,500 Fenway faithful was the fifth-inning kerfufle between Boston's Ben Chapman and Tigers catcher Birdie Tebbetts.

The Red Sox had score four runs—three of them coming on a home run by Foxx—to take a 4–1 lead. With no out and a runner on first, Chapman stepped up to the plate. Tebbetts shouted encouragement to pitcher Vern Kennedy while at the same time taunting Chapman, who went down on a called third strike. Tebbetts and Chapman exchanged words, followed shortly thereafter by a more physical spectacle.

The *Boston Globe* reported on the "untoward fistic interlude," suggesting the remarks between the combatants were inaudible to the crowd, but Charles Ward of the *Free Press* offered a fairly detailed dialogue. Whether that version of the conversation was real or imagined by the sportswriter remains a mystery.[7] Both Tebbetts and Chapman were ejected from the game. The Tigers battled, sustained by back-to-back pokes by Greenberg and York in the sixth inning and a two-run shot by York with Greenberg on base in the eighth to secure the victory.

Like Jake Powell, Chapman was an unrepentant bigot. "Men like [him], and there were a lot of men like him, hated my guts and resented my success all the more because I was a Jew," Greenberg wrote in his memoirs.[8] As manager of the Philadelphia Phillies in 1947, Chapman unleashed a volume of vitriol at Jackie Robinson, then in his rookie season, calling him every vile name in the book. In an interview decades later, Chapman sought to explain and even defend his actions.

> Oh, we called [Greenberg] "Kike." It was all part of the game back then. You said anything you had to say to get an edge. Believe me, being a southerner, I took a lot of abuse myself when I first played in New York. If you couldn't take it, it was a case of "if you can't stand the heat, get out of the kitchen."[9]

Chapman was correct, and as difficult as it may be to believe in today's PC environment, such tactics *were* the norm back in Greenberg's time. Some teams even went to the trouble of bringing up a minor leaguer for the express purpose of riding the Jewish player, knowing it wouldn't be a big deal if a busher got ejected from the game. Most of the time Greenberg stewed silently, but even this gentle giant had his limits.

In his 2001 memoir, *Sleeper Cars and Flannel Uniforms*, Greenberg's former Tigers teammate Elden Auker wrote, "Hank was an extremely tough guy, but he never showed that off. He wasn't one to lose his temper. He was probably the most highly respected player on the team."

But Auker, a pitcher who won 11 of his 21 decisions in 1938 employing an unusual "submarine" delivery, recalled one time when the normally placid Greenberg, outraged at anti-Semitic remarks hurled at him by an unidentified member of the visiting Chicago White Sox, took action after the game.

"He paid a visit to [their] clubhouse, looking to exact revenge on the cowardly, mouthy jerk from the other team," Auker wrote. Greenberg challenged the offending player to step forward but no one did. The White Sox players silently avoided his gaze in shame.[10]

From Boston, the Tigers traveled south to New York to take on the Yankees for a two-game series. Make that one game as rain washed out the scheduled meeting on Friday, May 6.

Joe DiMaggio, one of baseball's rising stars, was among a group of California athletes who signed a letter demanding the release of Baron Gottfried von Cramm, Germany's top tennis star and the second-highest ranking amateur in the world. Von Cramm had been arrested and sent to a concentration camp on what local authorities described loosely as "morals charges." Among other athletes who signed in support were American tennis greats Donald Budge and Helen Wills Moody.[11] On May 14, von Cramm was convicted of having homosexual relations with a Jew and sentenced to a year's imprisonment.

Meanwhile another "political" protest by the Non-Sectarian Anti-Nazi League called for a boycott of the Joe Louis-Max Schmeling fight, scheduled for June 22 at Yankee Stadium. Members of the League's women's division handed out pamphlets condemning the propagandist aspects of the event, a rematch of their June 19, 1936, battle that had also been hosted at the legendary ballpark.

Schmeling earned the victory that day in 12 rounds, knocking down the "Brown Bomber" in the fourth, the first time Louis had been sent to the canvas in his professional career. It was also one of just two knockout losses, the second coming some fifteen years later to Rocky Marciano when Louis was well past his prime.

Fans in the US were disappointed over the outcome but Adolf Hitler and his Nazi Party cronies were over the moon, heaping praise on the German champion and pointing to the result as proof of Aryan superiority.

News of the increasing struggles facing Jews in countries under the Axis powers slowly trickled in to an American audience over the course of 1938 but a disquieting number were not moved. Some editorials echoed the position of one that appeared in Greenberg's local newspaper. On May 9, the *Free Press* editors declared, "A problem has been created for the United States Government by the action of the German Government in issuing one-way passports to certain Jewish and other refugees wishing to migrate to this Country [sic]."

The article noted that "these one-way migrants would be persons without a country" and that "[T]he United States would be 'stuck' with them, whether they turned out to be desirable citizens or not." The piece concluded with a sentiment that represented a sizable portion of public opinion at the time: "While Americans sympathize with the victims of Nazi persecution, there is no reason for letting down the bars and admitting to this Country [sic] potential paupers or criminals who can't be returned, if occasion demands, to the country from which they came." In other words, we feel your pain, but this isn't our problem.[12]

It may not have been the 60,000–65,000 (depending on the source) that saw Lawrin win the 64th running of the Kentucky Derby, but more than 41,000 fans—the largest crowd of the season in the early going at Yankee Stadium—showed up for the May 7 game. Auker and Wade combined to give up nine runs on 11 hits and three walks in four innings, and there was no catching up in a 12–8 defeat. Greenberg was hitless in three official at-bats but received two of the seven free passes handout out by Yankees pitchers.

The quirky Boots Poffenberger offered his own take on just how tough it was to face the boys from the Bronx, not only on the field, but from the bench as well. "Those Yankees call you a lot of nasty names when you are pitching against them," he told Charles Ward. "The nicest thing they ever call a guy is a pig and they never call you a white pig or a spotted pig. It's always a black pig and a dirty one. They also put in a couple of extra words to help describe it."[13]

The Tigers lost their next game, too, 7–6 in ten innings to the host Philadelphia A's. Greenberg clouted his sixth home run to lead off the sixth inning and also belted a triple in five at-bats. But the bad weather pursued the Tigers like a hunter, cancelling their next two games in Philly.

The Tigers moved on to the nation's capital where they split their two-game series with the Senators. Vern Kennedy kept his 1938 record spotless with his fourth straight win as he scattered seven hits in the 4–1 opener, nudging the Tigers into fifth place. Greenberg drove in a run with a double in the second but was thrown out when he tried to stretch it into a triple and was tagged after sliding past the bag.

Despite the loss, Senators' owner Calvin Griffith credited the Tigers with providing a measure of incentive for his team, which ended the day tied with the Yankees for first place with a record of 15–8.

"This spring they walked all over us in exhibition games and I gave my boys a talking to," Griffith said. "I told them their showing against the Tigers proved that they were not in good shape, and every man buckled down and got himself in good condition. That is why we are winning."[14]

"Griff," as he was known to fans and reporters, also created a bit of controversy that season when he complained there was a difference between the balls used in the American and National Leagues.

Such ideas had come into question in the first several weeks of the season, with those used in the NL supposedly somewhat livelier than the AL counterparts. Griffith took advantage of his team's location by sending samples to the US Bureau of Standards for testing, but they found no discernable difference in performance. Since these weren't the results he wanted, Griffith declared the testing methods faulty and vowed to get to the bottom of things. "I figure that a good fungo hitter could tell whether there was any difference between the two balls," he told the press. "If he takes an honest swing—and I don't want a fellow who will not—I think we will find out that the National League ball, on the average, will travel farther than the American League ball. I'm sure of it."[15]

The Sporting News took up the situation on its editorial pages. In their May 19th issue, the paper stated "it has been found that there isn't much difference in the carrying property of the two [league's] balls," while at the same time saying "the National League type seems, if anything, to have more rabbit than the American sphere." *The Sporting News* pooh-poohed the allegations, deciding "A good hitter will slug any kind of ball" and that "[e]xperts can prove anything with theories of mechanical devices."[16]

On May 12, the Tigers lost the second game to the Senators, 7–6, despite Greenberg's seventh home run, a three-run shot that sailed into the left-field bleachers.

With the running of the Kentucky Derby completed, the general sports attention returned to the upcoming Louis-Schmeling rematch. Besides baseball, boxing and horse racing made for the most news on the sports pages in the days before even radio was a common household appliance. Newspapers frequently reported which celebrities—including ballplayers like Greenberg—could be seen at the track or a boxing match. Just about every rumor and aspect of the upcoming bout was made available to a readership anxious for something to keep their minds off their day-to-day problems, so these little items, sightings, and reports from the fighters' training camps were always welcome, even those that touched upon issues outside the actual sport.

In an effort to make the upcoming event somewhat more palatable to those who opposed the match on political grounds, boxing promoter Mike Jacobs pledged to donate 10 percent of the gate—estimated to be at least $7,500—to President Roosevelt's new foreign refugee movement. It was almost an offer that could not be refused, putting groups like the Anti-Nazi League in a no-win position. Oppose the event and you deny much needed relief; agree to it, and you are running counter to your mission statement.

The Tigers trudged back to Detroit, looking forward to the opportunity to get healthy against the last-place St. Louis Browns with their 6–17 record. Things got off to a good, if not easy, start in the series opener on Friday the 13th. George Gill gave up five runs on eleven hits and three walks, but his teammates were two scores better, thanks to some shaky defense by the Browns. Greenberg went hitless in four at-bats, but St. Louis skipper Gabby Street elected to walk him intentionally in the sixth inning after Gehringer had driven in a run with a double. That strategy backfired when Greenberg subsequently scored the go-ahead run in the 7–5 win.

The weather was once again an enemy as rain and unseasonably cool temperatures forced the cancelation of following day's game. Perhaps the ballplayers and fans took advantage of the break to take in the new swashbuckler film *The Adventures of Robin Hood*, starring Errol Flynn and Olivia de Havilland. One of the first Technicolor marvels, the epic tale of the man who stole from the rich and gave to the poor was the perfect fantasy for the time. Ironically, it was the most expensive production to that point for Warner Brothers, costing about $2 million. It proved a righteous investment, however, raking in $4 million at the box office. *Robin Hood* received four Oscar nominations including best picture of the year, losing out to the screwball favorite *You Can't Take It With You*, starring Jimmy Stewart, Jean Arthur, and Lionel Barrymore, another movie with a poor-but-happy versus rich-but-clueless theme.

Playing conditions weren't much better on Sunday, but the Browns and Tigers did manage to get in five innings, enough to make the game official. Unfortunately for the home team, they found themselves on the wrong side of the ledger with a 4–1 defeat. Greenberg went 0-for-2 with another walk. Detroit had two men on base in the sixth when the game was finally called. Since Greenberg had made the final out in the fifth, he wasn't in a position to make a contribution to put his team ahead.

But rain was the least of the team's problems. A bigger question lingered: what to do with Rudy York?

York was a slugging . . . ballplayer. There was not much else you could say. The Ragland, Alabama native made his debut at age twenty-one in 1934, appearing in three games and collecting one hit in six at-bats. After two additional productive seasons in the minors, the Tigers brought him back for good in 1937.

There was never any question about his offense; he had slugged 35 homers with 101 RBIs and a .307 average during his first full season. The question was where to put him in the field? In 1937, York appeared in 54 games behind the plate, 41 at third base, and another two at first. To say he was not overly skilled at any one spot would probably be kind. He had little talent (and, seemingly, desire) to improve his defensive skills. Too bad the concept of a designated hitter wasn't yet a gleam in anyone's eye he would have been a natural.

Cochrane was determined to make York his regular catcher, but with the team mired in second division—the bottom half of the league—the Type-A manager soon lost patience and benched York and his .269 batting average, three home runs, and 10 RBIs. In his stead, Cochrane substituted George Robert Tebbetts behind the plate for at least the immediate future. Tebbetts, a bright twenty-five-year-old from Burlington, Vermont, whose aunt bestowed his life-long nickname "Birdie," would go on to spend more than sixty years in the game as a player, coach, and manager, even earning a spot on the cover of the July 8, 1957 issue of *Time* magazine in his capacity as skipper of the Cincinnati Reds.

After the 1938 season, Greenberg agreed to move to left field so the relatively immobile York could be the regular first baseman. Greenberg's motives were not entirely altruistic: Tigers general manager Jack Zeller gave him a $10,000 bonus to give up his familiar post, pushing the slugger's salary to a robust $50,000. It turned out to be a great decision for everyone concerned: In 1940, Greenberg and York combined for 74 home runs and 284 runs batted in.

Goodbye, Brownies; hello, Senators. On May 16, Washington rolled into town for another two-game series. And look who's back in the lineup . . . and behind the plate, too! Rudolph Preston York, despite all those assertions by the manager about leaving him alone to adjust to the relative inactivity of the outfield.

York responded by hitting a grand slam in the sixth and driving in another run to lead the Tigers to a 13–7 victory before 8,000 appreciative fans. The Senators put up a fight, scoring five times in the eighth against Kennedy, but he managed to hang in to complete the game for his fifth win against no losses. Greenberg singled twice in four at-bats, drew a walk, and drove in a pair of runs.

The next day, however, brought more rain. That made five games in eleven days that had to be rescheduled. Maybe *that* was why the Tigers couldn't seem to get into any kind of groove.

The weather eventually cleared out but the losing ways lingered. They managed just one run on six hits—none by Greenberg, who grounded out to the pitcher with bases loaded in the third—in a 5–1 defeat.

Next up were the A's, who swung into Detroit for a three-game set. The Tigers won the May 19 opener, 6–2, with York and Greenberg each contributing two-run blasts. Greenberg's eighth long ball came in the sixth inning, sixth also being his spot in the batting order that day as he continued to struggle offensively. He had just one other official at-bat, walking in two other trips to the plate.

The seesaw continued the next afternoon with the Tigers falling to the A's, 5–2. Schoolboy Rowe was on the hill, making just his third appearance of the season. After averaging 20 wins in his first three full seasons (1934–36), he developed arm trouble and pitched in just ten games in 1937, mostly in relief. The 1938 campaign would be even more frustrating. The rust was apparent against the A's although only one of the five runs he allowed was earned: York, playing in left field, made an error in the ten that opened the floodgates. Greenberg had one of the team's five singles and also walked once.

The Tigers took the May 21 finale, 7–5, to close out the series. Greenberg once again went 1-for-3 with a walk, but scored twice as Kennedy won his sixth straight decision. The victory pushed the Tigers into fifth place with a 12–15 record.

Detroit made it two in a row on May 22, when Foxx and the Sox came to town. In the first inning, York blasted his second grand slam in a week, providing all the runs in the team's 4–3 win. Meanwhile, Greenberg's line in the box score—a hit and a walk or two—was becoming routine.

After one more rainout on May 23, the Tigers sustained a painful loss when Harry Eisenstat sustained a fractured skull from an errant ball that hit him in the eye during batting practice. Perhaps distracted by the loss of their colleague, the Tigers fell 5–4 in front of 6,600 fans the following day. Foxx untied his league lead with Greenberg by hitting a two-run shot in the seventh that ended up being the difference maker, as the Tigers came up a run short in the bottom of the ninth. Lefty Grove, who at 38 seemed to be improving with age, came away with his eighth straight win without a loss despite having some control issues: he walked eight batters—including Greenberg twice—while striking out just one. It was the 14th straight game in which Greenberg received at least one freebie, giving him 30 in 29 games.

Perhaps it was just braggadocio but despite his club's sluggish start, Cochrane told reporters he expected a logjam of teams contending for the pennant, "a six-club race right down to the wire in the American League with the Yankees meeting plenty of trouble before and if they repeat."[17]

The Tigers continued their win one/lose one pattern when they hosted those Yankees on May 25, thanks in part to Greenberg's first two-homer game of the season. The cloudy and wet conditions didn't dampen his powerful swing: the first shot went over the left-field screen while the second was a 420-foot missile to left-center off veteran knuckleballer "Poison" Ivy Andrews.

The two taters in the 7–3 win were part of his 4-for-4 day, which included a single and double, raising his batting average from .280 to .305. It also allowed him to regain the American League lead over Foxx, ten to nine.

His day's work, however, was overshadowed by York, who also hit two home runs—the teammates went back-to-back twice, in the third inning and again in the fifth—and drove in all of the Tigers' remaining runs. Perhaps they celebrated with a post-game cheroot and a belt: the *Detroit Free Press* advertised Phillies (no connection to the National League team), "America's Largest-Selling Cigar," at only a nickel while a pint of Irish American Whiskey went for just over $1. After all, Prohibition *had* been repealed five years earlier.

The May 26 game saw the Tigers revert to form, losing to the Yankees 5–1 with Greenberg cracking two more hits and driving in Detroit's only tally as Rowe lost once again. This would prove to be the last big league game of the season for the twenty-seven-year-old. His opponent, reliable Red Ruffing, hadn't pitched since May 8, the victim of a bout with the flu. Fully recovered, he struck out 10 and earned his fifth win against one loss.

Things started to turn around as the Tigers made their second trip to Chicago, sweeping the White Sox in the three-game series. After seven straight games in which he batted sixth in the lineup, Greenberg returned to his customary spot in the cleanup position. He responded by providing some early fireworks in the May 27 series opener, giving a thrill to the crowd of 6,000 (including 3,000 women who enjoyed the game gratis thanks to a Ladies Day promotion). With the bases empty and two out in the third, the Hammer unloaded on a Frank Gabler fastball. "Hank's clout was really a whopper," Ward wrote in his *Free Press* story, "the ball crossing a wall 15 feet in height and 440 feet from home plate."[18] It was the first time anyone had reached such a distance at Comiskey Park since the bleachers had been built in 1927.

Bad weather once again limited Greenberg's at-bats in Saturday's game, a 9–1 victory that was called after six innings. He had four plate appearances, going hitless in two official at-bats but scoring twice after receiving two of the dozen walks issued by Bill Cox and Merritt "Sugar" Cain, the latter of whom was released by the White Sox the following day.

The rain certainly cost Greenberg in this one. He grounded out to end the fifth with runners on second and third following a double steal. Two innings later, Tommy Bridges, the Tigers' starting pitcher and number nine batter, led things off with a free pass followed by a Billy Rogell single. Barring a double play, it's likely Greenberg would have come to bat at least one more time, but that's when the heavens opened up and the umpires called a halt to the proceedings.

The Tigers evened their record at 17–17, reaching the .500 mark for the first time all year, with a 2–1 win on May 29. Greenberg was 0-for-3 with another two walks against Monty Stratton, whose potentially brilliant career was cut short when he accidentally shot himself in the right leg while hunting following the season.

The Tigers returned to Briggs Stadium for a Memorial Day doubleheader against the Browns. They won the opener, 10–9, with Greenberg supplying what proved to be the winning run in the eighth inning with his 12th home run, a shot that went into the upper deck of the left-field pavilion. It was something of an atonement for his earlier shortcomings: Hitting in the cleanup spot again, he came to bat in the first inning with bases loaded and no one out but instead of getting the team off to a inspiring start, he took a called third strike. He did the same thing in the fifth with two on and one out.

The nightcap was less satisfying for the holiday crowd of 49,500: a 3–0 loss in which Greenberg managed two singles, accounting for one-third of the Tigers' entire offensive production.

Detroit closed out the month with a record of 18-18, thanks to its recent four-game winning streak. That was, however, unacceptable for a team that was predicted to contend for an AL pennant.

"As a result of the Tigers unhappy start, Detroit fans have been seeking the source and have succeeded only in generating a cross-current of dissension, smugness, laziness," wrote Sam Greene in the May 25 issue of *The Sporting News*. "Manager Mike does not presume to have the whole answer to his team's slow start but he is inclined to believe that the primary drawback was the protracted slump of Hank Greenberg, Rudy York, and Charlie Gehringer." Greene helpfully pointed out that, "Greenberg is hitting about 40 points below his average for 1937."[19]

The Sporting News—the "Bible of Baseball"—was a godsend for fans, offering news, statistics, and box scores for all professional baseball from the majors to the lowest of the minor leagues. That week's edition offered a special enticement for new subscribers. For only $4, they could get a year's subscription along with their choice of the new edition of the Spalding or

Reach Guide Book, which offered a thorough recap of the 1937 season. (But wait, there was more: a major league schedule to hang on their wall!) Not covered were the Negro Leagues, however, as they were outside the purview of "organized" baseball. The overall reporting in *TSN* was excellent, but the production process did take considerably more time; as a weekly publication, the information was slow in arriving and *two* weeks behind the times as far as statstics were concerned.

Greene may have had a point. Hammerin' Hank was once again leading the league in home runs and York had rediscovered his long ball power as well, yet on the aggregate their production had been disappointing. But what about the fact that the Tigers played 16 of their first 20 games on the road? Would they be able to catch up once they were able to fatten up on "home cooking?" What about all those games—five in May alone—that had been cancelled by inclement weather, as well as the May 15th loss that was called early?

Greene's analysis aside, Greenberg was starting to show signs of life, slowly shuffling off his early-season sluggishness. Between May 1 and 27, he raised his batting average 100 points and his home run total in 35 games was an even dozen, one more than Babe Ruth hit over the same span in 1927. But no one was really paying attention to the Detroit dynamo at that point.

While Greenberg had already established himself as a slugger since coming on the scene as a full-time player in 1933, it was under his own banner; he was not yet as a potential pretender to the figurative throne held by the Sultan of Swat.

In 1938, Ruth was winding down his illustrious career in almost shameful fashion: The Brooklyn Dodgers, a lackluster team that would finish the year with a record of 69–80 and in desperate need of a box office draw, offered him $15,000 to be their first base coach. He didn't do his managerial aspirations any good with his lackluster work ethic, unwilling or unable to grasp the intricacies of the team's signals. In addition, his long-standing antagonistic relationship with former teammate Leo Durocher—now a key member of the Dodgers and their future manager—did not bode well for an overall harmonious environment.

It was no secret that Ruth wanted to manage, and preferably the Yankees. He sought the job following the untimely death of Miller Huggins, who passed away suddenly at the end of the 1929 season as the result of a rare skin disease. But team owner Jacob Ruppert did not consider him anywhere near disciplined enough. "How can you manage a team when you can't even manage yourself?" the stern Ruppert asked Ruth. After Bob Shawkey led the team to a third place finish in 1930, the Yankees hired Joe McCarthy, who won eight pennants in fifteen full seasons at the helm. Both Huggins and McCarthy were inducted into the Hall of Fame for their success in the dugout.

Under a different alignment of the stars, however, Ruth might have been Greenberg's manager.

In 1933, Frank Navin wanted to do something to invogorate his team. The Tigers hadn't won a pennant since 1909. He also needed to get the fans out to the ballpark. He thought he might accomplish both goals by hiring Ruth as a player-manager.

By that point, the Sultan of Swat was 38, overweight, and in the sunset of his fabled career. The numbers he put up were still pretty decent for anyone not nicknamed "The Bambino," or any of the numerous sobriquets pinned on him by the sportswriters. Perhaps he had something left in the tank. Maybe a change of scenery would do him good. And wouldn't the Yankees welcome the chance to be rid of him and his salary, even if it wasn't the $80,000 he had earned in 1930, $5,000 more than President Hoover? (Ruth always joked that he deserved the dough because he had a better year than the Commander in Chief.)

After securing permission from Ruppert and general manager Ed Barrow, Navin contacted Ruth, inviting him to come to Detroit for an interview. But Ruth had already committed to a 13-day trip to Hawaii for some exhibition games and a golfing event. Could it wait until he returned to the mainland? No, said Navin. He wanted to wrap things up as soon as possible. Barrow counseled the living legend to change his plans, but Ruth being Ruth, he might have thought his reputation would support his ego and that Navin would accommodate his schedule. He was wrong. The Tigers owner was unimpressed by the combination of entitlement and a salary demand that was far above what he was willing to pay. Thus Ruth lost perhaps his one and only real managerial opportunity and the Tigers ended up hiring Mickey Cochrane.

Although there's no way of knowing what might have happened had Ruth been given the Tigers' reigns, there could be no complaint about Cochrane who led Detroit to a pennant in 1934 in his first season and a world's championship the following year.

Greenberg in May:

G	PA	AB	R	H	2B	3B	HR	RBI	BB	SO	BA	OBP	SLG
25	111	88	18	31	5	1	9	18	23	13	.352	.486	.739

Greenberg in 1938 (through May 30):

G	PA	AB	R	H	2B	3B	HR	RBI	BB	SO	BA	OBP	SLG
36	161	127	27	40	6	2	12	22	34	22	.315	.460	.667

Notes

1   Gordon Cobbledick, "Milnar Rescues Harder in 9th, Indians Beat Tigers, 4 to 3: Fans Greenberg for Final Out." *Cleveland Plain Dealer*, May 2, 1938.

2   James E. Doyle, "Meelnar—Like Shampeen." "The Sport Trail." *Cleveland Plain Dealer*, May 2, 1938.

3   Gordon Cobbledick, "Indians' 10 runs in 4th Capture 2d Series from Tigers: Weatherly Nabs 450-Foot Smash." *Cleveland Plain Dealer*, May 3, 1938.

4   "Pope Is Warned by Duce's Paper on Nazi Attack," *Brooklyn Eagle*, May 9, 1938.

5   The others include Joe DiMaggio, Yogi Berra, Stan Musial, Roy Campanella, Mike Schmidt, Barry Bonds, Alex Rodriguez, and Albert Pujols.

6   Tim Keefe, Cy Young, Christy Mathewson, Eddie Plank, Walter Johnson, Grover Cleveland Alexander, Rube Waddell, and Dazzy Vance.

7   Gerry Moore, "Tigers win odd game of series; fistic encounter enlivens contest." *Daily Boston Globe*, May 6, 1938; Charles P. Ward, "York's Homer Gives Tigers First Series in East."*Detroit Free Press*, May 6, 1938.

8   *Story of My Life*, p. 64.

9   Allen Barra, "What Really Happened to Ben Chapman, the Racist Baseball Player in *42*?" *The Atlantic*, April 15, 2013.

10 Elden Auker and Tom Keegan, *Sleeper Cars and Flannel Uniforms: A Lifetime of Memories from Striking Out the Babe to Teeing It up with the President* (Triumph Books, 2001).

11 "U. S. Sportsmen Demand Nazis Free von Cramm." *The New York Times*, May 7, 1938.

12 "We Shouldn't Fall For It." *Detroit Free Press*, May 9, 1938.

13 Charles P. Ward, "Bizarre Shouts of Yank Bench Irk the Baron." *Detroit Free Press*, May 8, 1938.

14 "Griffith Gives Tigers Credit for Nats' Rise." *Detroit Free Press*, May 12, 1938.

15 Charles P. Ward, "Ward to the Wise." *Detroit Free Press*, May 13, 1938.

16 "Reply to Lively Ball Arguments." *The Sporting News*, May 19, 1938.

17 "Diamond Dots." *Daily Boston Globe*, May 24, 1938.

18 Charles P. Ward, "Greenberg's Record Homer Gives Kennedy No. 7." *Detroit Free Press*, May 28, 1938.

19 Sam Greene, "Barbershop Critics on Cochrane's Neck." *The Sporting News*, May 26, 1938.

JUNE

"Baseball gives you every chance to be great. Then it puts pressure on you to prove that you haven't got what it takes. It never takes away the chance and it never eases up on the pressure."

—Joe Garagiola[1]

Hank Greenberg's first roommate in professional baseball was Joyner "Jo-Jo" White. "He was called Jo-Jo because of the way he pronounced his native state," Greenberg wrote in his memoirs.

[N]o two people could be more different than me, coming from the Bronx, and [him], claiming that he came from Atlanta. Well, we pinned him down, it was twenty-five miles out of Atlanta, a little town, Red Oak, Georgia, that didn't even show up on the map. Anyway, our relationship was terrific. We used to fight about the Civil War every night. Jo-Jo would say, "Why my granddaddy would chase your granddaddy right up the goddamn hill and run his ass off." I hated to tell him this would have been

53

impossible, as my granddaddy had been in Romania at the time, but that didn't keep Jo-Jo from carrying on.[2]

Several biographies describe a typical encounter between Greenberg and people like White, born and raised in small rural areas, like the story when the two were first getting acquainted in 1931 as members of the Beaumont Exporters, the Tigers' top minor league affiliate.

> At one point, Greenberg asked a gawking . . . White, "What're you looking at?" His teammate replied, "Nothing. I've never seen a Jew before. I'm just looking." Greenberg responded, "See anything interesting?" The fellow admitted, "I don't understand it. You look just like anybody else." "Thanks," Greenberg countered, thereby terminating the conversation. Later, Greenberg recalled Atlanta [sic] native White admitting, "Hell, I thought all those Jews had horns."[3]

In a 1980 interview as part of an American Jewish Committee oral history project in which thousands of people discussed the "Jewish experience" in the United States, Greenberg expanded on the story: "He didn't know what a Jew was. He just had heard the word and knew there were people like that, but, as far as he was concerned, I could have been Frankenstein, I mean that's what a Jew was supposed to look like."[4]

Following a scheduled day off on May 31, Greenberg and White took in the championship fight for the welterweight title between

Barney Ross and another "Hammerin' Hank," Henry Armstrong. Ross, who was at the tail end of his career, was another Jewish athlete who served as a heroic symbol to his people during tough times.

Ross was born Beryl David Rosofsky in New York in 1909. The family soon moved to Chicago where circumstances forced him to grow up a bit quicker after his father, a rabbi who also owned a vegetable store, was murdered during a robbery. Ross's mother had a nervous breakdown and while his three younger siblings were temporarily sheltered in an orphanage and later taken in by members of the extended family, he was forced into premature adulthood at age fourteen.

Ross learned how to box, as did so many other young men, Jewish or otherwise, as a means of survival on the streets. If you were good enough, perhaps you could make a living at it. Ross was more than good enough, losing just three of 81 professional bouts.

Also like Greenberg, Ross served during World War II. A marine who was wounded in the battle of Guadalcanal, he received the Silver Star for bravery in the face of combat and for saving the life of a wounded comrade.

Immigrant and first-generation Jewish parents were generally unhappy when their sons decided to pursue a sports career rather than the slower and steadier track that took the road through an academic career, including college. Such opportunities were rare in the *shtetl*, where both poverty and discrimination were plentiful. One of the reasons they risked leaving the familiarity of the "old country"—doesn't matter which country it might have been—to come to the United States, the *goldene medina* (Yiddish for "golden country") was to give their children the opportunity they themselves never had. Similar to the bible's description of Israel as the land of milk and honey, immigrants believed the streets in America were paved with gold. They soon found out otherwise. If they wanted a better life, getting that diploma and going into a profession was key. Those first-generation Americans who didn't live up to their parents' strict expectations were considered a *shande*, a shame to the family. That's one of the main reasons so many Jewish athletes, like Barney Ross, changed their names.

Many, but not all. In a 1928 article in *The New York Times*, Richards Vidmer wrote about Andy Cohen, a second baseman/shortstop with the New York Giants, who made the gutsy decision to retain the family name. Not that defiance, coupled perhaps with a sense of pride, were the only motives. There was also a marketing aspect.

The Giants made no secret that they were looking for a Jewish ballplayer—preferably a very good one if possible—that might draw more Jewish fans to the Polo Grounds. They thought they had their man in Mose Solomon—"The Rabbi of Swat"—who hit an astonishing 49 home runs for the Hutchinson Wheat Shockers of the Southwestern League in 1923. The Giants brought him up for two games at the end of the season in which he had three hits in eight at-bats, including a double. Unfortunately for the Giants, Solomon returned to the minors the following year and never made it back to the big leagues.

In a front-page item that began "Oi gevald! John McGraw finally has that Jewish ball player he has been looking for these many years," the *Sporting News* noted Cohen had "all the natural characteristics of his race—thick, dark hair, dark skin and keen mentality."[5] This was the accepted journalistic patois of that era: non-WASP players were often described in exotic terms. The press often referred to Rudy York and other Native Americans extraction as "Chief." Of course, they meant it in the nicest possible way. But perhaps the most famous example might be the profile of Joe DiMaggio in the May 1, 1939, issue of *Life* magazine: "Instead of olive oil or smelly bear grease he keeps his hair slick with water. He never reeks of garlic and prefers chicken chow mein to spaghetti," the popular newsweekly disclosed.

The Giants' strategy worked for a couple of years: Cohen had 14 home runs, 114 RBIs, and a .281 batting average in 262 games. He was sent to the minors where he could stay sharp with steady playing time but, like Solomon, Cohen never returned to the majors, the victim of a broken leg he sustained the very day he was informed he was being sent back up to New York. (It wasn't just Jewish *athletes* who were concerned about bias. Dan Daniel, like Vidmer, a popular and respected sports journalist, was actually born Daniel Margowitz but changed his surname out of fear of anti-Semitism and discrimination.)

The Tigers resumed their schedule with a 13-game road trip, completing a tough stretch of 15 out of 17 played away from the embrace of their hometown fans. They opened a four-game series against the Yankees in the Bronx on June 1.

Ballclubs used to travel by train in those days. The time spent together on the long rides, coupled with the lack of today's diversions, brought some players closer together, giving them time to discuss their profession. (A trip from Pennsylvania Station in New York City to the LaSalle Street Station in Chicago on the 20th Century Limited took 16 hours in 1938. The Tigers made a trip like this at the beginning of September.) Reporters traveling with the teams also benefited, managing to find the players with their guard down, sharing a meal or drinks or card game with them. They had a lot more in common than their modern-day counterparts, especially on an economic level.

On the one hand, Greenberg enjoyed coming back to New York. His father had earned a good living and was eventually able to buy the Acme Textile Shrinking Works. The family moved out of Greenwich Village to a 16-room house across the street from Crotona Park, Hank's home away from home.

As a youngster, he had grown to six-feet by the time he was thirteen. While he found his size something of an embarrassment among his smaller classmates, it sure came in handy during his athletic pursuits. He became a local legend, playing baseball, basketball, and soccer—which he considered his best sport—at James Monroe High School, whose other celebrity alumni include cartoonist Jules Feiffer, jazz great Stan Getz, actor Danny Aiello, and Ed Kranepool, one of the original New York Mets and the kid who broke Greenberg's home run record at the school.

Greenberg frequently brought teammates home for what must have been (for the overwhelmingly majority) their first taste of kosher cuisine, including his mother's gefilte fish. But he never stayed there; it would have been too much of a distraction with intrusive but well-meaning family, friends, and neighbors wanting to hear stories of his adventures and pestering him with endless questions. He preferred to board with the team at the art deco New Yorker Hotel in midtown Manhattan.

On June 1, Greenberg hit his 13th homer in the opening game against the Yankees. The ball flew into the left field stands to put the capper on the Tigers' 8–4 win which put them over the .500 mark for the first time all season.

That minor accomplishment was negated the next day when the Tigers dropped both games of a twin bill, 5–4 and 5–2. Greenberg went a combined 1-for-7, driving in one of Detroit's runs in the second game with a double in the third inning to temporarily knot the score at 2–2. He was also hit by a pitch in the opening game for the first time all year.

Baseball is a game of territory. Just as football teams strive to keep opponents out of their half of the field—and certainly out of the end zone—one of baseball's goals is to protect the plate. For pitchers, that often means throwing inside to prevent the opposition from getting too comfortable in the batter's box. Some of them developed reputations as "head hunters," more than happy to give the batter a "shave." Sal Maglie, who pitched for ten seasons in the majors, earned the nickname "The Barber" for his propensity to throw high and inside. Interestingly enough, he averaged fewer than six hit batters per season over his career.

For all the perceived animus against Greenberg because of his religion, he was actually not hit that often. In nine full and four partial seasons, Greenberg was plunked just 16 times. Of course, there is no way of knowing how many times he was sent flying to the dirt to avoid a high hard one. In his memoirs, he recalled one incident in particular:

For some reason I was looking for a curveball and the pitcher just wound up and fired one behind my head.

Well, I did duck, but not far enough out of the way of the ball, and it hit the button on top of my cap. I don't mind telling you I turned white; I realized then that my career could very well have ended right there and how lucky I was that I hadn't been beaned. It was the only time I ever came close to being beaned in all the years that I played.[6]

After losing two of three to the Yankees, moving along to Boston extended Detroit's increasing sense of futility. Greenberg was hitless in four at-bats on June 4, while Jimmie Foxx provided most of the offense for the home team. His two home runs—a three-run blast in the first to open the scoring and a solo in the third—guided the Red Sox to a 5–3 victory, dropping the Tigers back down to three games under .500.

Vern Kennedy managed to keep his record perfect, winning his ninth game the following afternoon to snap the team's four-game losing streak. By the end of the second inning it was all over but the playing: the Tigers scored nine runs in the second inning and didn't look back, completing the 10–4 pasting without much in the way of contribution from Greenberg, who had one hit and walked twice, scoring a run and swiping his third base on the back end of a double steal. He reached base twice in the fateful second frame, leading off the festivities with a single and drawing a base on balls when his turn at bat came around again.

The Tigers lost a heartbreaker in the June 6 series finale thanks to a questionable call by an umpire and a subsequent lapse on defense. With Detroit leading 7–6 going into the eighth, Boston catcher Gene Desautels singled off the wall in left, but fell down rounding the bag. Gehringer's relay from outfielder Chet Laabs seemed to catch the runner scrambling back to first as Greenberg slapped on the tag, but umpire Bill Grieve "was not looking at the play with Tiger eyes" and called Desautels safe.[7] That gave the Sox the opening they needed. A sacrifice moved Desautels to second. The next batter, Doc Cramer, lofted a fly to Pete Fox in right who badly misjudged the ball before letting it clank off his glove, sending the tying run across the plate. In the ninth, Bobby Doerr drove in the game-winner after another misplay put runners at first and second with one out.

With Rudy York working behind the plate and going 2-for-3, the Tigers didn't really miss Birdie Tebbetts, who was given the day off to attend his brother's wedding back in Nashua, New Hampshire. "Until you have seen George (Birdie) Tebbetts in formal morning attire, you simply have not lived," he told the *Free Press* playfully the day before. "I am, to put it modestly, a honey."[8]

Next up for the Tigers was a three-game set against the A's in Philadelphia. The good news: the Tigers took two of three. The bad news: Greenberg was 0-for-8 with one RBI in the first two games—5–4 and 5–1 victories—and 2-for-4 with a run scored and an RBI in the third game, an 8–5 loss and the first defeat for Kennedy. Philadelphia rookie Dario Lodigiani had the game of his life on June 9, going 4-for-4 with a grand slam and a total of five RBIs off the usually reliable hurler, who allowed seven runs on six hits and five walks. In fact, it was the only time that Lodigiani would have five RBIs in a game for his career.

Hammer-less Hank had now gone a week without a home run. In the interim, Foxx had caught up and passed him for the

AL lead with 18, thanks to a power spree where he collected seven in six games. Losing 7 out of their last 11 games, the Tigers hoped to turn things around when they visited the struggling Washington Senators. While the team showed signs of life, winning in 10 innings, 7–6, when York's pop-up dropped in for a bloop RBI double, Greenberg went 1-for-5. Harry Eisenstat picked up his first AL win on the strength of four shutout innings in relief.

Ward's eponymous column in the June 11 *Free Press* was devoted to the elephant in the room: Greenberg's batting slump. In the Tigers' 46 games, "Large Hank," as Ward called him, had driven in an undistinguished 27 runs, which, if he maintained that rate, would put his season's total at roughly half of the 184 he accumulated the previous year. Of course, Ward had no way of knowing what lay ahead. We, on the other hand, have the benefit of hindsight.

One also has to wonder about the possible role of Greenberg's religion in Ward's commentary. The writer referred to the ballplayers decision "a long time ago . . . to make himself the greatest Jewish star the game has known." Is that so? Although there was no denying his religious identity and his readiness to stand up to those who would disparage his people, Greenberg did not go around wearing his Judaism on his sleeve. He said in numerous interviews during his playing career and well afterward that he never wanted to be known as a great Jewish player, but rather a great player who happened to be Jewish. Semantics? Perhaps. But in Ward's era it was quite common to refer to—if not state outright—a player's ethnic background as if it was "proof" of the athletes' persona and performance. (As another example of what would now be considered politically incorrect: In his game report for the same day, Ward wrote that "5,000 Ladies Day fans among the gathering of 12,000 squealed their dismay" in the home team's loss. Because obviously men don't squeal, they yell lustily.).

Ward suggested Greenberg was too concerned about the presence of York, worried that the young slugger, who often batted ahead of him in the lineup, would drive in the runs that in that past were "rightfully" his. If York succeeded, Greenberg's opportunities were minimized. If York failed, Greenberg felt extra pressure to get the job done, lest Cochrane start thinking about changing the situation and rearranging the batting order again. Had the team been performing to expectations instead of playing peekaboo with the .500 mark, perhaps their skipper would have left things alone. But two months into the season, perhaps it was time to try a few new things.

According to Ward, the Tigers' skipper suggested Greenberg would be wise to adopt a new philosophy at the plate, taking a page from his Tiger antecedent Ty Cobb and just concentrate on getting singles instead of going for the long ball.[9] Can you imagine? "The Hammer" a singles hitter? Several years later, Ralph Kiner, Greenberg's protégé while they were with the Pittsburgh Pirates, famously said, "Singles hitters drive Fords. Home run hitters drive Cadillacs." (We'll overlook the inadvertent insult at Henry Ford's famous products.)

With almost a third of the season complete and the team doing so poorly, Cochrane was worried about his own situation. His nerves became frayed as he sought to exert more discipline on this charges in an attempt to make them buckle down and concentrate. For example, he fined pitcher Boots Poffenberger, the team's resident colorful character, $100 for breaking curfew. (The press took delight in referring to the second-year hurler from Williamsport, Maryland, by his full name—Cletus Elwood Poffenberger—because it sounded so regal; he was often called "the Baron" on second reference.) And York was still giving Cochrane fits as he continued to figure out the most efficient place to put him on the field.

The bigger diamond news that June 11 was provided by Cincinnati Reds pitcher Johnny Vander Meer, a twenty-three-year-old from Prospect Park, New Jersey. In his tenth start of the year and twentieth of his career, he tossed a 3–0 no-hitter against the Boston Braves with just three walks standing between him and perfection.

Greenberg developed a reputation as a clotheshorse (*The New Bill James Historical Baseball Abstract* named him the "Best-Looking Player" of the 1930s). Eisenstat credited Greenberg with schooling him on how to act like a big leaguer off the field, in addition to giving him advice on the playing aspects. "[H]e showed me how to dress. He used to wear quality clothes, and I remember he used to wear Sulka ties, which cost about $35 or $40 even in those days."[10]

On June 12, the Tigers were losing to the Senators in Washington 11–1 going into the sixth inning. In his memoirs, Greenberg told a story about owner Walter Briggs getting a shave at the Detroit Athletic Club while listening to the game on radio. Briggs told his barber that if the team came back to win, he would buy each player a custom-made suit. It seemed like a safe bet at the time. In fact, it turned out to be an expensive proposition— but one Briggs was probably tickled to pay off—as the Tigers scored 10 runs in the sixth and seven more in the ninth to take an unlikely 18–12 victory.

"Sure enough, after we won and got back to Detroit, we got a note from the management that Mr. Briggs was ordering each of us a suit of clothes from his private tailor," Greenberg wrote. "In those days, to be sent up to get a suit of clothes made to order, which few of the players had ever had, was a big deal. . . . The prices of the suits then were about $125 each, a fortune."[11] I wonder of either Greenberg or Briggs ever thought to stop in Detroit's landmark Landsburgh's Department store? For $25, he could have picked up a suit with two pair of trousers off the rack in the "air cooled men's shops" and maybe top it off with a Hanley Hall chapeau from the nearby Sidney West shop for an additional $7.50.

Nowadays, any game-used clothing or equipment can bring a nice price on the memorabilia market. But even during the Depression you could find someone willing to part with an exorbitant amount of money for the chance to own something that had once belonged to a professional athlete.

Cleveland Indians pitcher Johnny Allen was fined $250 for walking off the mound after umpire Bill McGowan told him to remove a "ventilated shirt" he was wearing in a game against the Red Sox. Allen, the third man in the Tribe's rotation behind Mel Harder and Bob Feller, sold the jersey to Higbies, the city's biggest department store, for a reported $500.[12]

June 13 was an open date on the schedule for the Tigers. However, they did not have the opportunity to enjoy the day. Owners were always looking to make an extra buck, so the team traveled to West Virginia for an exhibition against their Class C affiliate, the Charleston Senators of the Middle-Atlantic League. The Tigers beat their juniors, 7–1, in front of 1,800 fans thrilled at the prospect of seeing the big-time stars they might have only ever read about. York provided all the runs his team needed with a double and a long homer. Greenberg was 0-for-3 but reached on an error, stole a base, and scored a run. Even Cochrane got into the act. He played first base for the sixth, seventh, and eighth innings, then donned the tools of ignorance for the final inning behind the plate for the first time since he sustained his skull fracture in 1937 and the last time as a player.

A three-quarters-page advertisement placed by General Mills for their iconic Wheaties in the *Free Press*' the next day highlighted the upcoming series between the Tigers and A's. Players from both clubs were featured in the promotion, including Greenberg, who was the only one actually shown with a bowl of the "Breakfast of Champions," chowing down while supposedly poring over the *Free Press'* sports section. "Homerun-hitting Hank Greenberg is a great favorite throughout the league," the copy proclaimed. "Fans everywhere like his clever play and drive! And Hank Likes Wheaties! 'A big bowl of Wheaties every morning,' the clouting Bengal confides, 'is the Greenberg way to start the day.'"[13]

Perhaps if his teammates had similarly eaten a nutritious breakfast, they might have not lost the June 14 opener, 8–2. Greenberg supplied the only power, smacking a two-run homer—number

14—in the eighth off Lynn "Line Drive" Nelson. In his game recap, *Free Press* sportswriter Don Holst noted the fickleness of some 6,000 school children in attendance.

"The boys and girls had been booing Greenberg up to that time, so Hank, who is more concerned about his failures than anyone else, became pale mad," wrote Holst. The blast "was a terrific line drive that struck the upper deck in left. It was still carrying upward when it struck the grandstand."[14]

That ended a twelve-game stretch without a home run, which would be Greenberg's longest power drought of the season. But the scarcity continued over the next two games against the A's, a 7–6 loss on June 15 followed by a 12–3 win the next day. Cochrane dropped Greenberg to sixth in the order again and moved York and Pete Fox up to the fourth and fifth spots, respectively. York stepped up to the challenge with three RBIs, a double, and his 16th home run, moving him two ahead of Greenberg.

"By dropping Greenberg a few notches in the batting order, Cochrane seemed to have done Hank and the club some good," wrote Ward. "Hank looked better with the pressure off him, made two singles and scored three runs. A couple more days like that and the troublesome slump will be a thing of the past."[15]

The news about Greenberg and the Tigers was welcome, but it paled in comparison with one of the more dramatic moments in professional sports history.

Sports pundits and fans love to hash over which records will last forever. They said no one would ever come close to Gehrig's consecutive games-played mark, but Cal Ripken Jr. proved them wrong in 1995. Every time a batter goes more than 25 straight games with a hit, they start talking about "The Streak," Joe DiMaggio's 56-game run in 1941. So taking that "never say never" attitude, who can say if some pitcher won't come along and break Johnny Vander Meer's accomplishment of June 15 when he tossed his second consecutive no-hitter? This one came in a 6–0 win against the Brooklyn Dodgers in their first night game at Ebbets Field. And while Vander Meer didn't allow a safety, he did walk eight batters, including three in the bottom of the ninth with just one out before getting a force play at the plate and a fly ball from Leo Durocher to seal his place in the history books.

Did the nocturnal nature of the game have anything to do with the outcome? After all, both sides had to play under the same conditions. Didn't seem to bother the Reds too much. This was just the second night game in the major leagues, coming more than three years after the Reds beat the visiting Philadelphia Phillies, 2–1, at Crosley Field on May 24, 1935. It was such a momentous occasion that President Roosevelt switched on the lights at the Cincinnati ballpark via a remote control from the White House.

Although not common, night games had been an experiment in the minors, which struggled to come up with new ideas to keep the fans coming out during the Depression. Since it was implausible that those who were fortunate enough to have jobs in the small towns that made up the bulk of the bush leagues would dare take time off during a work day, night games seemed like a natural progression, even if it took some time to get the quality of illumination right.

Back in the Detroit daylight, the Tigers split a June 17 double-header against the Senators, dropping the opener in a 12–10 slugfest before winning the nightcap, 4–3. Greenberg went without a hit in the first game but made up for it with three in the second, including his 15th home run that traveled into the upper deck of the left-field bleachers, the first time anyone had done that at Briggs Stadium.

Prior to the game, Bucky Harris, the Nats' manager, had a few choice words to say about the previous week's suit-winning game. "Some day the Senators are going to beat the Tigers so disgracefully that Mr. Briggs will go right down to the clubhouse and take those $125 suits away from them and we'll beat them out of their shirts just to rub it in."[16]

Greenberg homered again the following day, helping Eisenstat win his first start of the season as the Tigers beat the Senators, 5–3. Number 16, a solo shot into the left field pavilion in the second inning, gave Detroit a 3–1 lead and tied him with York for the team lead.

His momentary joy might have been tempered by the fact that the Tigers had released his younger brother, Joe, from their Toledo Mud Hens farm club on May 22. Back in April, Irv Kupcinet—who years later became a renowned columnist for the *Chicago Sun-Times* as well as a talk show host and radio personality—was a bit off the mark when he told sports fans in the *Sentinel,* a Jewish communal newspaper, "Don't be surprised to find Joe playing third base for Detroit next year." Sadly, it was not to be.[17]

There have been over 350 sets of brothers in the major leagues; Hank and Joe were not among them. But it wasn't for lack of trying.

The Tigers, perhaps hoping to have lightning strike twice, signed Joe in 1936 and assigned him to the Charleston Senators, their Class C affiliate in the Middle-Atlantic League. After his release from the Mud Hens, he signed with the Baltimore Orioles, a team in the International League with no major league affiliation. He also played for the Johnstown Johnnies in the same circuit. Statistics are very sketchy for that era, but BaseballReference.com lists him as playing for six teams over five seasons, never advancing past the Class A1 Fort Worth Cats in 1941 (that would be the equivalent of AA in today's minor league system).

Hank went to bat for his kid brother, so to speak. "Hank believes anybody can do as he did if only he wants to badly enough," wrote Ward in his January 4, 1938, column. "His attitude on this subject was revealed when the Tigers were looking over his brother Joe to see if he showed enough talent to warrant their giving him a contract.

"'Oh, I don't care how much skill he shows,' said Hank impatiently one day when somebody wondered aloud if Joe would make the grade. 'I know he has ambition and that is all he needs. That is all I had when I started.'"[18]

Not exactly. Hank also had the talent, raw as it was when he was first starting out. Joe, not so much.

Hank Greenberg may not have been the model for Superman, but there have been plenty of allusions to the Man of Steel and the Jewish/immigrant experience.

Jerry Siegel and Joe Shuster, a couple of Jewish teenagers in Cleveland, Ohio, created the iconic character in the early 1930s. It took several years from putting their ideas down on paper until their hero made his debut in DC's *Action Comics* #1 in June 1938.

Collectively, Siegel and Shuster *were* Clark Kent, their super-hero's alter ego: bookish, bespectacled, and deferential. Their fantasy has been common among nerds since time immemorial. They wanted acceptance and to make a difference (they also wanted to save the day and get the girl but in their day-to-day personae that was not going to happen).

The same could be said about the Jewish population: *they* wanted acceptance, *they* wanted to be brave and strong . . . but anti-Semitism was their kryptonite.

Will Eisner, the genius behind *The Spirit* and other iconic comics, spoke for his contemporaries when he said, "I knew I was Jewish in the same sense that any American knows he was Irish-American or Italian-American. It influenced me in that the stories I grew up hearing were the stories told in Jewish families, but I never thought about being Jewish when I did my work."[19]

Nevertheless, most superheroes came from other worlds, aliens who in many cases felt compelled to hide their true identity for safety concerns.

Larry Tye, author of *Superman: The High-Flying History of America's Most Enduring Hero*, contributed a list of "10 Reasons Superman is Really Jewish," to the *Forward*, a Jewish publication based in New York, in 2013. Among them, a comparison between the infant Superman and the prophet Moses:

> The alien superbaby was not just a Jew, but also a very special one. Like Moses. Much as the baby prophet was floated in a reed basket by a mother desperate to spare him from an Egyptian Pharaoh's death warrant, so moments before Kal-El's planet blew up, his doomed parents tucked him into a spaceship that rocketed him

to the safety of Earth. Both babies were rescued by non-Jews and raised in foreign cultures—Moses by Pharaoh's daughter, Kal-El by Kansas farmers named Kent—and all the adoptive parents quickly learned how exceptional their foundlings were. The narratives of Krypton's birth and death borrow the language of Genesis. Kal-El's escape to Earth is the story of *Exodus*.[20]

While it is documented that Hall of Fame Yankees catcher Yogi Berra was a devotee of comic books, it is not known whether Greenberg had any similar interest or, if he did, whether he caught on to any Jewish connection between Superman and Jews.

With the Tigers in fifth place with a 28–28 record, a day off on June 20 gave Ward a chance to reflect on "What is wrong with the team? That is what Mickey Cochrane would love to know." Yet for all the problems, the *Free Press* scribe saw a silver lining.

"A hopeful sign is the fact that Hank Greenberg seems to be emerging from his batting slump," Ward wrote. "The Tigers need Hank. Up to a few days ago he was trying for home runs while his team mates [sic] told him to try for singles and that the home runs would take care of themselves. Now Hank has begun to try for singles and is hitting home runs."[21]

In the same issue, the *Free Press* alerted readers that they could "Get the Complete Story of the Louis-Schmeling Fight," coming two days hence. The match was taking on almost comic book proportions in the depiction of good versus evil as the boxers prepared for their rematch.

In addition to the interest on a purely sports level, there were political ramifications that had been absent in the previous fight. On June 11, Shirley Povich, who spent more than seventy years writing for the *Washington Post*, devoted most of his column to the simple logistics of the bout, noting that the book was 8–5 against Max Schmeling, who was eight years older than Joe Louis. In the custom of the day, Povich referred to them as "the German" and "the Negro," respectively.[22]

Meanwhile, the Tigers split a doubleheader with the visiting Red Sox. York handed out two more souvenirs to tie Foxx for the AL lead while Greenberg didn't have as good a time, going hitless in seven at bats.

"When Umpire [Bill] Summers called Hank out on a bad strike in the eighth inning of the second game, Big Henry exploded," wrote Ward in his "Tiger Notes." "When he went to the dugout he tossed the bats all over the place. It was the first time he had shown any temperament since joining the Detroit club."[23]

Perhaps purged of the ignominy of failing in the previous game, Greenberg launched a three-run rocket, No. 17, to cap a five-run first inning for the Tigers on June 22. Foxx kept pace, hitting his 20th; York remained at 19, having hit one in each game of the recent twin bill.

Coverage of the Tigers' 8–3 win was small fry in comparison to that of of Louis's victory over Schmeling, which took up half the front page of the *Free Press* on June 23. The fight lasted just two minutes and four seconds, with the "Brown Bomber" sending his opponent to the canvas three times before Schmeling's trainer tossed in the towel in front of 80,000 screaming spectators at Yankee Stadium.

Celebrations were reported in Paradise Valley, a business and entertainment subsection of Detroit's Black Bottom district where Louis lived, a neighborhood that was home to a predominantly African American population within the city. Across the Atlantic, the reaction was more somber. "All over the Reich they had clustered in homes, restaurants, and cafes to hear the fight they had hoped would bring the world championship to Germany," according to an Associated Press story. The audience, which tuned in about 2 a.m. local time, reportedly included Adolf Hitler.

"Schmeling's . . . pals said their only comment was an echo of what the German announcer said at the close of his broadcast from the Yankee Stadium ringside.

"'We sympathize with you, Max, although you lost as a fair sportsman. We will show you on your return that reports in foreign newspapers that you would be thrown into jail if you lost are untrue.'"[24] Not exactly putting out the welcome mat.

The Tigers closed out their series with the Red Sox with a 10–2 win, highlighted by homers from York (his 20th, tying him with Foxx), Chet Laabs (his seventh), and Greenberg (number 18), whose blast "was the best of the afternoon," according to Ward. "It rocketed into the upper-deck of the right field pavilion at the 375-foot mark."[25]

Up next: the New York Yankees. Greenberg made a point of greeting the enemy at their hotel, the Book-Cadillac, and "like a little boy, taunted the Yankees as they came to town," wrote Doc Holst in the *Free Press* on June 24. "'I just want to shake hands with some guys who are hitting worse than I am,'" said the ballplayer.

"A guy named Gehrig and another named Joe DiMaggio seemed to blush as they piled from their cabs.

"'And,' continued Little Boy Greenberg, 'tell that Vernon [Lefty] Gomez he'd better warm up all night in the hotel lobby or even I will get a hit against him.'"[26]

True to his word, Greenberg slammed a pair of homers the next day—one off starter Spud Chandler, the other against reliever Steve Sundra—to help the Tigers claim a 12–8 win, their fourth in a row to put them three games over .500 for the first time all year. Greenberg now had four long balls in his last three games and six over his last nine, putting him in a three-way tie for the league lead with Messrs. York and Foxx.

Greenberg also walked three times, the first one an intentional pass in the opening inning to load the bases. But that strategic move failed, as Chet Laabs followed with a single to bring in two runs. The other two base on balls might have been the Yankees being extra cautious—and rightly so. His first homer—good for three runs—traveled 450 feet to the back of the bullpen in left-center. The second, with one man on in the eighth, went into the upper deck in left field. "This one was hit even harder than the first and probably would have gone over the pavilion or at least bounced off the roof if it had not been held back by the adverse winds," penned Ward in his coverage.[27]

Writing for *The New York Times*, John Drebinger emphasized the "devastating force" of Greenberg's blows. The second homer "enabled the Detroiters to win going away. It left the Yankees with nothing better to do than stick around until tomorrow."[28]

Ward's *Free Press* colleague, Doc Holst, gave credit to an unlikely source: the batboy.

"Joe Roggin . . . is really the genius who has pushed Big Hank back on the pleasure path. Joe is Hank's greatest admirer and the feeling is somewhat mutual . . .

"'Oh, Hank will be O.K. from now on. I got him out in the park in the morning these last few days and now he's all loosened up. He feels swell again,'" said young Joe.[29]

Greenberg was hitless the next day, but the Tigers tied a major league record by hitting a home run in their fourteenth straight game. Unfortunately it wasn't enough, as they still fell to the Yankees, 9–3.

The local sports naysayers, fronted by Ward, were out in force after another loss to the Yankees on an unseasonably chilly and overcast Sunday, which delayed the start time by an hour.

Ward pointed out that the Tigers had won just one series during their current homestand, dropping two and tying another. "That is hardly pennant-winning ball," he wrote. "So unless there is a change the boys can start planning fall hunting trips right now. The World Series will not interfere."[30]

The Tigers dropped the next game, too, but the disappointment was somewhat mitigated by the announcement that four members of the team had been named to the American League All-Star squad: Greenberg, Gehringer, Kennedy, and York.

The "midsummer classic" was the brainchild of Arch Ward, sports editor for the *Chicago Tribune* (and no relation to the *Free Press'* Charles P.) as part of the Windy City's 1933 Century of Progress Exposition, pitting the best in each league against each other for bragging rights (the players received no additional pay for appearing in the games). The AL took three of the first four meetings, with Gehringer and Lou Gehrig the only players who had been on each roster since the first All-Star Game.

It was Greenberg's second selection and while it was certainly an honor, he was still smarting from the 1937 game in which he spent the whole affair on the bench as Gehrig played the entire game at first base. Although, to be fair, he did live up to the designation of "All-Star" by driving in four runs with a home run and a double to lead his temporary teammates to an 8–3 victory. Foxx, the third first-sacker on the AL squad, grounded out as a pinch-hitter; Greenberg just stewed on the pine. So he could be forgiven if he wasn't that enthusiastic about the tribute in 1938.

Even in the All-Star Game's infancy, pundits and players complained about the selection methods and who should make such decisions. In the early stages, managers voted for the players. As the Tigers moved into Cleveland for their next series, Ward noted that the Indians and their followers were miffed that *their* first baseman, Hal Trosky, had been overlooked while Greenberg and Gehrig made the team even though they were having sub-par years. As of Ward's story datelined June 28, Trosky was batting 65 points higher than Greenberg and 82 points better than Gehrig.

"If you are going to name a committee of managers to pick a team you concede at the start that the abilities of the players cannot be determined by the averages. If they would then why go to the trouble of appointing a committee?" Short answer: records are deceptive, but "only a Clevelander would pick Trosky" over a Gehrig or a Greenberg, Ward wrote.[31]

Hank didn't hit a homer in the Tigers' 5–4 loss to Trosky and the Indians, but little brother Joe did for the Orioles, providing the game-winner in their 4–3 win over the host Newark Bears. The next day it was the older Greenberg who came through.

Hank found himself promoted in the batting order, moving up to fifth behind York. He justified Cochrane's decision by providing a three-run blast in the eighth inning to give Detroit a 4–3 come-from-behind victory over Cleveland. The wallop earned special mention by the *Plain Dealer*'s James Doyle:

> "Mr. Greenberg though as happy as a squirrel in a nut house on his return to the Jungle Cats' dugout, comported himself with most becoming modesty . . . 'Was that a hit you mugs," he asked his admitting mate, 'or was that a HIT'?
>
> "Keep it in caps, Mr. Printer . . . That's just where it belongs."[32]

As Greenberg's 21st of the season flew off his bat, "20,000 customers put their hands over their eyes and said 'Ow!'"[33]

The number of patrons at League Park paled in comparison to the 77,000 that filled Cleveland Stadium, the Indians' weekend home, for the closing event in the 49th annual supreme council convention of the Mystic Order Veiled Prophets of the Enchanted Realm, a fraternal organization that flooded the city with some much-need bonhomie (and cash).

Greenberg caught up to Foxx the next day with his 22nd home run, a solo shot off a shaky Bob Feller that went deep into the left-field stands. The Indians nearly blew a 9–3 lead, forced to stage a comeback in the bottom of the ninth for a 10–9 win. That dropped the Tigers back to .500, bringing their season's record to 33–33.

Even though Greenberg had raised his batting average to an even .300 and slugging percentage to .640—outstanding production from just about anyone else in the league—he was basically treading water in the opinions of fans, media, and even Tigers management. The adage goes that home runs come in bunches. He hit one on June 1 and had to wait until the 14th for his next. Then he hit six more between June 22 and 30. Coming to the midpoint of the season, the whispers about a Greenberg-Ruth connection were slowly growing louder.

Greenberg in June:

G	PA	AB	R	H	2B	3B	HR	RBI	BB	SO	BA	OBP	SLG
30	132	110	29	30	2	2	10	25	20	18	.273	.389	.600

Greenberg in 1938 (through June 30):

G	PA	AB	R	H	2B	3B	HR	RBI	BB	SO	BA	OBP	SLG
66	293	237	56	70	8	4	22	47	54	40	.295	.428	.641

Notes

1 H. A. Dorfman and Karl Kuehl, *The Mental Game of Baseball: A Guide to Peak Performance* (Diamond Communications, 2002), p. 201.

2 *Story of My Life*, p. 46.

3 Robert C. Cotrell, *Two Pioneers: How Hank Greenberg and Jackie Robinson Transformed Baseball—And America* (Potomac Books, 2012), p. 29.

4 Henry B. Greenberg Oral History Memoir, William E. Wiener Oral History Library of the American Jewish Committee at the New York Public Library (digitalcollections. nypl.org/items/47eab380-0361-0131-9b19-58d385a7b928).

5   "Playing the Percentage." June 17, 1926.

6   *Story of My Life*, p. 105.

7   Charles P. Ward, "Tiger 'Daffiness' Play Costs Fifth Defeat on Trip." *Detroit Free Press*, June 7, 1938.

8   "Tiger Notes." *Detroit Free Press*, June 5, 1938.

9   Charles P. Ward, "Ward to the Wise." *Detroit Free Press*, June 11, 1938.

10 *Story of My Life*, p. 104.

11 Ibid, p. 100.

12 "$500 Shirt!" *Washington Post*, June 11, 1938.

13 "Athletics Arrive for Battle!" *Detroit Free Press*, June 14, 1938.

14 Doc Holst, "Macks Duplicate String-Shattering Victory over Kennedy." *Detroit Free Press*, June 15, 1938.

15 Charles P. Ward, "York's 16th Homer Helps Bridges End A's Spree." *Detroit Free Press*, June 17, 1938.

16 Doc Holst, "$125 Gift Suits Provide Bucky with Fight Talk." *Detroit Free Press*, June 17, 1938.

17 Irv Kupcinet, "Another Greenberg." *Sentinel*, April 28, 1938.

18 Charles P. Ward, "Ward to the Wise." *Detroit Free Press*, January 4, 1938.

19 Gerard Jones, *Men of Tomorrow: Geeks, Gangsters, and the Birth of the Comic Book* (Basic Books, 2005), p. 130.

20 Larry Tye, "10 Reasons Superman Is Really Jewish." Forward. com, June 12, 2003 (forward.com/culture/178454/10-reasons-superman-is-really-Jewish).

21 Charles P. Ward, "Some Days Tigers Are This, Some Days That." *Detroit Free Press*, June 21, 1938.

22 "This Morning with Shirley Povich." *Washington Post*, June 11, 1938.

23 Charles P. Ward, "Tiger Notes." *Detroit Free Press*, June 21, 1938.

24 "Nazis Promise Maxie Will Not Be Put in Jail." Associated Press, *Detroit Free Press*, June 23, 1938.

25 Charles P. Ward, "York's No. 20 Helps Tigers Return to Fist Division." *Detroit Free Press*, June 24, 1938.

26 Doc Holst, "Yankees Heckled by Greenberg as They Hit City." *Detroit Free Press*, June 24, 1938.

27 Charles P. Ward, "Tigers' 22 Homers in 13 Days Write New Marks." *Detroit Free Press*, June 25, 1938.

28 John Drebinger, "Battle of Homers Won by Tigers." *The New York Times*, June 24, 1938.

29 Doc Holst, "Tiger Notes." *Detroit Free Press*, June 24, 1938.

30 Charles P. Ward, "Tigers Fall to Lower Division as Homer Streak Ends." *Detroit Free Press*, June 27, 1938.

31 Charles P. Ward, "Ward to the Wise." *Detroit Free Press*, June 29, 1938.

32 James E. Doyle, "Hankus Sank us!" *Cleveland Plain Dealer*, June 30, 1938.

33 Charles P. Ward, "Homer No. 21 for Greenberg Takes Tribe Measure." *Detroit Free Press*, June 30, 1938.

JULY

"I know what I'm getting paid for. Unless I can keep hitting those home runs, I can't stay in that big money."[1]

—Hank Greenberg

Hank Greenberg's salary for 1938 was $30,000, a bit more than $500,000 in 2016 dollars or just about the major-league minimum these days. And he had to fight to get a $5,000 raise over the previous year, which he considered his best season: 40 home runs, a major league–leading 184 RBIs, and a slash line of .337/.436/.668. But this was a time before free agency, when players were bound by a "reserve clause" that made them the property of the teams with which they signed until they retired or were traded, sold, or released. And there were always hungry youngsters waiting in the wings, ready to step in and take a roster spot—even in Greenberg's case. Sure, a player could hold out for more money, but he was taking a big risk.

This was especially true during the Depression. There was an issue of public perception that management liked to hold over a player's desire for a raise, no matter how well-deserved it might have been.

The average salary for a lawyer in 1935 was $4,272. For doctors it was $3,695, while college professors might have expected to draw $2,666. Industrial workers pulled down about $1,200. Farmers—many of whom had seen their crops decimated by hostile climatic conditions, including the famous dust storms—were on the low end of the scale, barely pulling in $300 per annum. How would they react to someone holding out for thousands of *additional* dollars when they had a difficult times literally just trying to live from day to day?[2]

President Roosevelt signed the Fair Labor Standards Act in June 1938, setting a minimum wage, a maximum number of hours per work week, and limits on child labor, among other things. The legislation was actually enacted in October of 1938, but it would take some time before workers would see the benefits and perhaps use a little of that extra money into leisure activities such as going to a ballgame.

Even though the recovery had slipped due to the 1937 recession, baseball actually saw record attendance in 1938. Writing for the Associated Press at the end of the season, Hugh Fullerton gave Greenberg a nod as one of the reasons:

"Add together that exciting National League pennant race, the Yankees' slow start in the American League, the unusual interest aroused by such individual feats as Johnny Vander Meer's two no-hit pitching performances and Hank Greenberg's threat to break the home run record and you arrive at the fact that major league baseball attracted more fans during the 1938 season than ever before."[3]

Unfortunately, Greenberg's hometown supporters were unable to join in the fun. The Tigers would see their attendance drop from 1,072,276 in 1937 to 799,557, the largest decline in the league but still the second highest total attendance in the AL.

Despite all the threatened negative publicity, baseball fans seemed willing to give Greenberg and his co-workers a little extra latitude.

"There should have been resentment toward these men, who were making a good living by playing a boy's game at such a difficult time. Just the opposite was true," according to Joe Falls, a veteran sportswriter for several Detroit newspapers. "The fans, needing an outlet from all the worries of the day, embraced them as heroes. At least they could go to the ballpark and know there was still some normality in the world.

"An afternoon at Navin Field, with Gehringer shooting a double into the right-field corner and with Greenberg, up next, putting one into the left center-field bleachers, was a reason to feel good," he continued, referring to the previous name of the Tigers' ball park. "It was a reason to feel hopeful, too; if the ball club could survive, why couldn't the people of the city? The banks could close, but not the ballpark."[4]

When Greenberg arrived in Detroit for his first full season in 1933, he lodged at the Wolverine Hotel for $8 a week. "They gave you a room with a bed but no closets. . . . [W]e just hung our clothes on the curtain rod in the bathroom," where players could save a few bucks on cleaning bills by using the shower to steam their clothes.[5]

He also recalled what passed for extravagance in those days: dinner and live music at the Leland Hotel, a nice twenty-minute walk from the ballpark (and where he resided during the season in subsequent years), cost $1.25. Plus the twenty-five cent tip he might leave to impress an attractive waitress.

The Tigers began July with a rare Friday off. When play resumed, they were in St. Louis to take on the perennially hapless Browns who were resting in their customary spot in the AL basement, already 20 games behind the first-place Indians.

Perhaps there was something special in the beer manufactured at the local Anheuser-Busch brewery, but that weekend the Brownies swept the visitors including both games of the July 3 doubleheader. They outscored Detroit 25 to 12; Greenberg had a hand in three of the Tigers' runs, scoring two and driving in one.

Could his lack of production be the lingering result of his old wrist injury? That was the "official" reason (or excuse, depending on the source) he used to back out of the All-Star Game, scheduled for July 6 at Crosley Field in Cincinnati. Tiger officials confirmed that Greenberg would undergo tests at Henry Ford Hospital in Detroit during the three-day break, but Greenberg himself said it wasn't really the limb that was the problem. Rather, it was his eyesight.

"Greenberg said that he believed recent poor timing at the plate may be caused by eye strain," and claimed he would be visiting an eye specialist rather than going for X-rays on his arm, according to an item in the July 2 *Free Press*.[6] Such theories aside, many believed Greenberg was still nursing a grudge over not being used in the All-Star Game the previous year, spending the afternoon on the bench watching Lou Gehrig play all nine innings.

Ballplayers were extremely sensitive when it came to eyesight and those with any visual weakness were considered lesser men. Eliot Asinof, himself an ex-minor leaguer, published his novel *Man on Spikes* in which the main character, Mike Kutner, was continually bypassed during his entire professional career because

he wore glasses. Some literary and historical analysts have interpreted that "glasses" was a code for "Jewish." In fact, Asinof—also
the author of *Eight Men Out*—used his friend Mickey Rutner, a
Jew who played in the minors for ten years and appeared in 12
games in 1947 for the A's, as the inspiration for Kutner.

At least one superstar made a concerned effort to protect his
eyesight. Rogers Hornsby, the irascible Hall of Fame second
baseman for the St. Louis Cardinals, Chicago Cubs, and a few
other teams from 1915–37, refused to go to the picture shows.
"If you want to be a great hitter, don't go to the movies—it ruins
your eyes," said the last National Leaguer to hit over .400. Then
again, he also advised ballplayers to avoid reading for the same
reason.[7]

A number of ballplayers heeded Hornsby's counsel regarding
the movies (and reading). If so, they missed out on a number of
classics that came out in 1938. Like sporting events, the cinema
offered people a chance to escape their problems for a few hours.
For twenty-five cents (a nickel or a dime for kids) you could sit in a
magnificently appointed "air-cooled" theater at a time when practically no residences featured such a luxury. The price of admission
often bought you a feature film with stars like Clark Gable, Joan
Crawford, Spencer Tracy, and Shirley Temple, among others; a "B"
movie (the theatrical equivalent of the minor leagues); a serial (*The
Lone Ranger*, *Dick Tracy*, and *Flash Gordon* were among the most
popular that year); and maybe a cartoon and a newsreel.

There were a number of genres from which to choose.
Screwball comedies poked fun at the rich, showing them to be
pampered airheads unaware of the plight of the common man.
These eccentrics generally had come away with valuable life les-
sons by the end of the story. Fred Astaire and Ginger Rogers took

viewers to fantasy worlds in glitzy musicals. Gangster pics were also terrifically trendy during the Depression. Many of those protagonists—played by the likes of James Cagney, Humphrey Bogart, and Paul Muni—found themselves forced by circumstances to turn to a life of crime to provide for their families with the bankers and businessmen portrayed as the bad guys. "The gangster's fearless tenacity helped viewers hold on to the idea that, regardless the odds, individuals might still somehow shape their own destiny," wrote Morris Dickstein in *Dancing in the Dark: A Cultural History of the Great Depression*. But as those stories progressed, these desperate men lost themselves to the seductive world of violence, fast women, and fancy living. In accordance with the Motion Picture Production Code, which had rules on everything from language to sex to violence, they would ultimately find their comeuppance lest some members of the audience think that crime actually paid.

If staying away from the cinema halls was one ritual among a subset of athletes, so was the superstition of not disrupting routine during a hot streak. Even though Greenberg went without a home run in the St. Louis series, he wasn't about to give up on a crucial part of his wardrobe.

The first half of the twentieth century was a much more formal period, even during hard times. In the larger cities, men often wore suits and ties, women wore dresses and gloves, and just about everyone wore a hat. Baseball was a business, which made the ballplayers businessmen, and their bosses expected them to present a good company image. In his "Game Notes" at the outset of the series with the Browns, Doc Holst noted in great detail the color and fabric of a specific Greenberg fashion accessory.

> Mr. Henry Greenberg, the Bronx sartorial flash, asks his many friends to bear with him in a neckwear dilemma. He wants these friends to please believe he has more than that one tie he has been wearing for the last two weeks.
>
> "Honestly, I've got two ties," the grinning Hank told other Tigers at lunch. "But I started to hit home runs again the first day I wore this tie and I gotta to [sic] keep it up until I go a few days without home runs. . . . All the boys are volunteering to help Hank tie it after every ball game in the hope of absorbing some home run virus.
>
> "If I get two home runs in the St. Louis series, I intend to sleep in it and even take my shower with it on," Hank told Bill Rogell, who was hinting that he would like to borrow the tie.[8]

One other long-held, if somewhat unscientific, theory was that the team in first place on July 4 would win the pennant.[9] That's what the Indians were hoping when they arrived in Detroit for their Independence Day doubleheader. Such holiday twin bills were coveted by club owners who knew they would draw a larger-than-average crowd. The schedulemakers tried to be equitable in handing out the hosting assignments, but in some cases it made more financial sense for a good club with a smaller ballpark to visit a less successful one with a larger one in order to receive a greater portion of the gate. And, then as now, more people meant more hot dogs, sodas, beer, programs, and other souvenirs, even if one ticket then covered both games, unlike today's business plan of charging for separate admissions.

The Tigers celebrated the day by claiming their independence against the Indians' oppression, taking both ends of the double-header to bring their head-to-head record to 4–7. Holst wrote about a freakish hit credited to Greenberg in the third inning of the opening game. It was "the highest and the shortest . . . of the day. . . . The ball went straight up, the wind finally bringing it fair. [Indians first baseman Hal] Trosky lost it in the sun or maybe in the clouds and the ball fell safely a few feet away from the plate for a freak single."[10]

Amusing episode aside, Greenberg had failed to hit a home run in five straight games. Time for some new neckwear?

The Tigers completed the unofficial first half of the season in fourth place at 35–36, 8.5 games behind the Indians and the Yankees with the Red Sox in third. Foxx led the AL in home runs with 23, with Greenberg second at 22, while Foxx was tops in RBIs with Greenberg in fifth place.

On July 6, the National League won the All-Star Game, 4–1. Rudy York came up as a pinch hitter in the seventh inning with the bases loaded and two out and terminated the threat by striking out against Mace Brown of the Pittsburgh Pirates. One can only imagine what impact Greenberg might have had. As it was, he spent the break relaxing and taking some extra batting practice.

Greenberg's participation—or lack thereof—in the recent All-Star Game was the subject of speculation. At the time, the *Sentinel's* Irv Kupcinet surmised that the higher-ups in the American League had actually asked Greenberg to sit this one out because they already had Lou Gehrig and Jimmie Foxx on the roster and wanted an additional pitcher instead of a third first baseman.

"[D]id Hank have an injured wrist," Kupcinet asked in his "Our Sports World" column in the July 14 edition? "If so, nobody knew about it, not even Hank. Did Hank withdraw? If so, nobody knew about it, not even Hank. . . . When questioned about the surprise move, Hank was bitter and refused to discuss the situation." (In his memoirs, Greenberg said it was a combination deal: His wrist *was* still hurting *and* he wanted the time off.)

Maybe Greenberg's Sulka tie just needed a few days off, too. When the schedule resumed on July 8, The Hammer hit his 23rd home run, a solo shot in the first game of a doubleheader, a 7–5 triumph over the visiting White Sox. He connected for two more, driving in three runs in Saturday's 4–0 win, and another on Sunday in a 5–4 loss. Of Greenberg's Saturday spoils, Ward wrote the first was a "regulation poke into the left field stands," but that his 25th—which now led *both* leagues—was "a blue-ribbon blast of 420 feet that split some of the woodwork in the center-field pavilion."[11]

His home run in the loss the next day drove in two runs, but the recent barrage still didn't move lift the Tigers higher than fifth place.

From one set of hosiery to another, the Tigers traveled to Boston for three games against the Red Sox. Greenberg did not homer in any of them.

Lefty Grove, one of the Tigers' chief nemeses, was the winner of that last game, a 12–1 decision, but banner headlines in the *Free*

Press the next day augured the end of the road: "Grove's Career Feared Ended as Arm Goes Dead."[12] In his 17-year career, Grove earned exactly 20 percent of his wins—60 out of 300—against the Tigers against just 19 losses (the only team against which he had a better record was the one he was currently pitching for). He kept Greenberg pretty much in check, holding him to just three home runs, 11 RBIs, and a .242 batting average in 70 mano-a-mano meetings. But rumors of Grove's professional death were somewhat exaggerated. Although he played in just five more games in 1938, the future Hall of Famer came back the following year to lead the AL in earned run average and went on for another two (albeit less productive) seasons before retiring at the age of forty-one.

After going hitless in a rain-shortened 3–0 loss to the host Yankees, Greenberg collected his 27th and 28th home runs over the next two games—also losses to the Bombers. His solo shot on July 16 came in the eighth inning, but he came up short in the ninth, hitting a fly ball to center with a runner on base after the Tigers had scored twice that inning. The next day featured a 16–3 blowout, so his two-run homer—again coming in the eighth—didn't make that much of a difference . . . especially after the Yankees scored eight in the bottom of the inning.

That made four losses in a row for the Tigers and six in their last seven, dropping them five games under .500. No wonder Cochrane was eating his spleen. "Prediction: The Tigers will not lose Monday. It's an open date on the schedule," Ward wisecracked in his "Tiger Notes" column on July 18.[13]

Ward devoted his writing on that off day to a rumor that one of the St. Louis ball clubs might be heading to Detroit. The Cardinals were in seventh place in the NL and the Browns were dead last in the junior circuit.

"It is true that the Motor City is the best baseball town in the country," Ward wrote, "But there is such a thing as too much baseball. And most cities that have two teams seem to have too much baseball."[14] The situation was even more pronounced during the Depression. In this case, he was referring to the Phillies and A's in Philadelphia, the Red Sox and Braves in Boston, and the White Sox and Cubs in Chicago; New York, with the largest population in the country, was able to support the Yankees, Giants, and Dodgers, even in these down times.

Wheaties took advantage of Greenberg's renewed output by running another advertisement in the *Free Press*: "Six feet four of lean, supple strength. Two hundred ten pounds of split second coordination. That's Hank Greenberg," the copy read, attributing his prowess no doubt to healthful benefits of their wholesome product.[15]

While the Yankees were moving on to the nation's capital, Max Schmeling finally returned home to Germany. The *Free Press* carried a photo of the defeated boxer accompanied by his wife, the Czechoslovakian-born actress Anny Ondra. The caption pointed out that only a small crowd came out to meet the couple upon their arrival in Bemerhaven and seemed surprised to find him walking under his own power, given the dire reports of his injured back and kidneys.

In one of his more thoughtful columns of the season, Ward wrote about the travails of "Swatto" and "Clonto," a couple of Tiger players who had sought raises from the team's late owner, Frank Navin, a few seasons earlier. There was no way to hide that

Greenberg was the former. Swatto approached Navin with the impression that he should get a pay increase because of all the runs he had driven in. Navin countered that of course he drove in runs; look at all those great players in the lineup ahead of him. How could he *not* have a lot of RBIs? Of course, the Tigers' owner said pretty much the same thing to Clonto, who scored a lot of those runs. How could he *not* score with someone like the powerful Swatto backing him up?[16] Ward's purpose here was to show the folly of basing a player's contract solely on statistics, which were often outside an athlete's effort and control. Why not have the manager submit daily reports on the players and use those as the criteria, he suggested?

Prior to free agency, the owners were well within their rights to cut players' salaries for poor or even mediocre performance, something unheard of today when the average salary for even a utility player today could be higher than an entire league's payroll in 1938. Following the 1957 season, the year after Mickey Mantle led the AL in home runs, RBIs, and batting average—winning the Triple Crown—the Yankees wanted to cut his wages by $5,000 because he failed to repeat such lofty numbers. The front office tried to convince their players that it was a privilege to be a member of such a successful and historic franchise and that the bonuses they regularly received for appearing in the World Series were practically a part of their salary. That should serve as enough incentive to do well.

On July 19, still on the road, the Tigers dropped to sixth place after falling in the opener of their series with the Senators in ten innings, 4–3. Cochrane returned Greenberg to the cleanup spot where he remained, save for one afternoon, for the rest of the season. They dropped the following two games as well, giving them a 1–8 record on their current road trip with two games in Philly on the way.

On July 21, a day after an AP story revealed that Bob Feller was afraid of potentially causing serious injury if he were to hit a batter, Rudy York was beaned by a Monte Weaver fastball that sent him first to the dirt and then to Garfield Hospital. League rules dictated that because of the death of Ray Chapman in 1920, any batter hit in the head had to be carried off on a stretcher as a precautionary measure. X-rays revealed York might have sustained a fractured skull.

The incident brought up nightmarish images for Cochrane, whose own playing career was brought to a screeching halt by a near-fatal beaning just the previous season. Fortunately, York was not as seriously injured as feared, although he did require a number of stitches. He was back in action nine days later.

In addition to losing a productive member of the team, the Tigers dropped the game as well, stretching their losing streak to seven games and falling deeper into panic mode. In that rain-soaked affair on Wednesday, Cochrane removed starting pitcher Boots Poffenberger after just four Senators came to bat. The breaking point came when Poffy didn't cover first base on a ball hit to Greenberg, allowing the batter to arrive safely. The Baron left the clubhouse before the game was over, courting insurrection and earning an immediate trip back to Detroit to await his fate while the Tigers finished the road swing.

"The club is not going so good now and I guess Mickey had to have somebody to blame it on," Poffenberger told reporters.

"I'm not sore. I guess I deserve it." He also warned he would not accept a demotion to the minors: "The salary I'm getting now is not enough."[17]

The gloomy weather followed the Tigers around like the cloud over Joe Btfsplk, a character in the popular comic strip *L'il Abner* who was generally known as the worst jinx in the world. Rain forced the cancellation of both the July 22 and 23rd games against the A's in Philadelphia, necessitating a doubleheader on Sunday.

With little else to write about, the *Free Press* featured a photo of a dapper Rudy York—sporting two-toned shoes, suspenders and a vest, and wearing a white bandage around his head—being helped into his suit jacket by an amenable nurse. The injury revived calls for some sort of protective skullcap to reduce the chance of serious harm in the future. It took another seven years until the Dodgers became the first team to adopt a form of head-gear, which was based on helmets worn by jockeys. Other ball clubs were not so cautious, however; batting helmets as we know them today did not become mandatory until 1971.

Ward attributed the high, inside pitches that conked York and other batters to an odd factor: fear by pitchers. They were "genuinely afraid of being killed with the batted ball," he wrote. "With the situation as it is, it would be best for all players if they wore the skullcap," presumably meaning they would also be used by teams in the field.[18]

Following the rainouts in Philadelphia, Greenberg hit his 29th home run in the first game of the July 24 doubleheader to help the Tigers break their seven-game chain, 7–6. Under cloudy skies and before a Sunday crowd of just 6,000 fans, Greenberg cranked a towering grand slam in the fifth inning off Nelson Potter, his third home run of the season against the A's hurler.

Detroit Tigers (left to right) Schoolboy Rowe, Cletus "Boots" Poffenberger, and Hank Greenberg in front of the screen at Fenway Park. (Photo courtesy of the Boston Public Library, Leslie Jones Collection)

Detroit Tigers (left to right) Leon "Goose" Goslin, Charlie Gehringer, Greenberg, and Billy Rogell pointing their bats at the field from the dugout steps at Fenway Park. (Photo courtesy of the Boston Public Library, Leslie Jones Collection)

Greenberg and Tigers teammate Lynwood "Schoolboy" Rowe standing on the dugout steps at Fenway Park. (Photo courtesy of the Boston Public Library, Leslie Jones Collection)

Heavyweight boxing champion Joe Louis throws a jesting punch at Greenberg. (Photo courtesy of the *Detroit News* Staff)

Boston Red Sox Jimmie Foxx and Greenberg crouching in front of the screen at Fenway Park. (Photo courtesy of the Boston Public Library, Leslie Jones Collection)

An unknown Detroit Tiger collides at home plate with Boston Red Sox catcher Rick Ferrell while Greenberg (then wearing uniform number 7) and home plate umpire Harry Geisel look on at Fenway park in a 1933 game. Note the proximity of the photographer on the left. (Photo courtesy of the Boston Public Library, Leslie Jones Collection)

Wheaties ads featuring Greenberg that appeared in the *Detroit Free Press* on June 14 and July 19, 1938. (Used with permission of General Mills Marketing, Inc.)

HILLERICH & BRADSBY CO.

INCORPORATED

SOLE MANUFACTURERS OF THE CELEBRATED

"LOUISVILLE SLUGGER" BASE BALL BATS

436 FINZER STREET

LOUISVILLE, KY.

AGREEMENT

In consideration of One Dollar ($1.00) and other good and valuable considerations in hand paid, and receipt of which is hereby acknowledged, I, the undersigned, hereby give and grant unto Hillerich & Bradsby Co., a corporation of Kentucky, its successors and assigns, the sole and exclusive right for Twenty (20) years from date, the use of my name, autograph, portrait, photograph, picture, initials and/or nickname, for trade-mark and/or advertising purposes in connection with the manufacture and/or sale of baseball bats, and I hereby consent to the registration thereof as a trade-mark for baseball bats by said Hillerich & Bradsby Co.

I hereby endorse and have bona fide used or will so use the bats, having my name associated therewith, as above authorized, and warrant that I have not previously made any agreement in conflict with the foregoing authorization.

EXECUTED in duplicate this *8th* day of *Sept*, 19*34* at

Detroit Mich

Henry Greenberg (SEAL)

Henry "Hank" Greenberg

WITNESS:

Henry Morrow

J. A. Hillerich

Detroit B.B.Club
$25.00 & 2 bats
9/10/34

Henry Greenberg

Professional bat contract signed by Greenberg with Hillerich & Bradsby Co., 1934. (Used with permission by Louisville Slugger Museum & Factory ®)

Front and back of Greenberg's professional bat order record. (Used with permission by Louisville Slugger Museum & Factory ®)

Left: Greenberg standing alongside Lou Gehrig. Greenberg had the opportunity to sign with the New York Yankees but declined when he realized Gehrig would be playing first base for quite some time. (Photo courtesy of the National Baseball Hall of Fame Library, Cooperstown, NY)

Below: Greenberg standing with an aging Ruth, showing each other how they hold a bat, circa 1947. (Used with permission by Louisville Slugger Museum & Factory ®)

Statue of Hank Greenberg that stands in the outfield of the Detroit Tigers home park of Progressive Field. (Photo courtesy of the Detroit Tigers)

After a scheduled day off, the Tigers returned home for the first time in over two weeks, and were met by 4,000 fans when their train pulled into Union Station on the morning of July 26. Perhaps that gave them an emotional boost as they proceeded to sweep the visiting Senators in three games (after being swept by them a few days before). Greenberg cracked two solo home runs in the opener—his 30th and 31st—to lead his mates to a 6–5 win in front of 68,000 appreciative fans in the series opener. The first one cut into the Senators' lead, bringing the home team to within one at 4–3. The second went into the upper deck in left at Briggs Stadium to break a 5–5 tie. In his recap for the *Washington Post*, Shirley Povich wrote, "First man at bat in the eighth, [Greenberg] ignored the first pitch but not the second. He sent the ball soaring over Al Simmons' head and the Nat's left-fielder took one fleeting glance at the hit and remained stationary in his tracks as the bleacher denizens scrambled for the ball."

Povich also noted "The Tigers had a mighty Hebrew combination today in Greenberg, the boy from the Bronx, and Harry Eisenstat, a left-handed lad from Brooklyn." Eisenstat, who had relieved starter Vern Kennedy in the sixth inning and shut the visitors down for the rest of the game, picked up his fourth win in seven decisions.[19]

It was at this point that the press began to take notice of his recent power surge and put it in historical perspective: "Hank's No. 30 and 31 Put Him Near Ruth Marks," the *Free Press* proclaimed in their headline on July 27. The paper also carried a photo "The G-Men United Again," featuring Gehringer and Greenberg flanking former teammate and current Senator Goose Goslin.

The Tigers resurgence shared space in the *Free Press* with an older topic: the Germans had put their own spin on June's heavyweight championship fight, editing footage of the match to make Joe Louis look like a cheating bully in his defeat of their beloved Max Schmeling. John Roxborough, one of Louis's managers, sent a telegram to Hugh Wilson, America's ambassador to Germany, to protest the screening of films there. "Joe won fairly and squarely," wrote Roxborough, "and he certainly isn't deserving of being placed in a bad light before the German boxing fans or anyone else." He accused the Germans of cutting in scenes from the first match between the combatants to give the impression of a Schmeling advantage. "Out of the same spirit and sportsmanship that Joe Louis always has shown in the ring, I am sending this cable asking you to protest the showing of the film." Roxborough wrapped up, "The boxing fans of Germany are entitled to know the truth. They are not getting it with the showing of the patched-up picture."[20]

Greenberg's pair of long balls came in his final two at-bats on Tuesday's match-up with Washington. Next day, same story with one difference: his 32nd and 33rd home runs came in his *first* two trips to the plate. Those four home runs in consecutive at-bats equaled the mark set by Foxx in 1934; only 28 hitters have matched that since 1938. The *Free Press* featured a large photo of Greenberg toweling himself off, undoubtedly satisfied after a productive day's work. The paper also published "The Saga of Hammerin' Hank," a list of each home run that included the date, pitcher, city, and number of men on base.

Greenberg's first shot in the 9–4 win—which moved the team back into fifth place—came in the initial inning off Senators starter Monte Weaver following singles by Rogell and Gehringer. His second came in the next frame with Gehringer on first courtesy of reliever Pete Appleton. Povich wrote in his beat story, "In comparison, his first inning clout was a bunt. That second homer climbed all the way into the upper deck in center field where the sign reads '400 feet.'

"Greenberg made a shambles of the ball game with his pair of productive clouts," he continued, "and is now seriously threatening the home-run record of Babe Ruth. At this date in 1927 . . . he boasted, like Greenberg, 33 of the four-base swats." But, Povich pointed out, "on the basis of games played [Greenberg] is ahead of Ruth's pace." Ruth had achieved that number in 93 games while Greenberg had needed just 88.[21]

Povich expanded on the occasion in his "This Morning" column in the same issue.

"[I]f anybody is to eclipse the Babe's mark . . . that fellow is more likely to be Hank Greenberg than anybody else." The scribe classified the slugger as a "guess hitter," someone who makes a presumption of what the next pitch might be and commits. If he's wrong, he can look awfully foolish. But if he guesses right, the ball can go a long, long way. Greenberg was never thrilled with that categorization and almost considered it an insult. He worked hard to get to this point in his career, taking extra batting practice as often as possible.

Povich pronounced that if Greenberg could set the record, "it will be an accomplishment far greater than Ruth's" because, as the scribe suggested, most of the stadiums of the era were friendlier to lefties like Ruth. At the same time, "Yardage means little to Hank when he connects. The four home runs he hit in the last two days here would have been homers in any ballpark in the league."[22]

Greenberg's bat cooled off the following day as he managed just a double and one RBI in four at-bats as the Tigers completed the sweep of the Senators, 12–4, which was their fifth straight win.

The five consecutive wins increased to eight as the Tigers won the first three of their four-game set with the visiting A's. With the team rolling, Greenberg remained on fire: he socked two homers and drove in four in a 9–2 win on July 29 and added two more in a twin-bill the next day, one apiece in 10–7 and 8–7 decisions, driving in three and two runs, respectively. In the first game of the doubleheader, the Tigers came back from a 6–1 deficit by scoring four runs in the seventh and five more in the eighth.

What made the final two games of the month even more noteworthy was that Eisenstat, the Tigers' other Jewish player, earned both victories.

In the opener, Detroit was down 5–0 after five innings. Eisenstat came on in the eighth after his mates stormed back with a run in the sixth and four more in the seventh to narrow the gap. Greenberg iced the affair with a three-run blast into the upper deck in left field, which made a winner out of the righty from Brooklyn.

As the icing on the cake, Eisenstat also tossed the final two innings in the nightcap, getting credit for his second victory of the afternoon when Greenberg hit his two-run job in the bottom of the eighth.

A photo of Greenberg with his arm around Eisenstat bearing the title "An Unbeatable Combination" was prominently displayed the next morning on front page the *Free Press'* sports section. Manager Cochrane warned the team in the celebratory clubhouse, "Fellas, lock yourselves in your rooms tonight because the Jews in Detroit are going to go crazy."[23]

As a co-religionist, Greenberg had a special affinity toward Eisenstat, offering not just the usual words of wisdom a veteran might pass along to a greenhorn but supplementing it with suggestions meant to help the younger man survive in a profession that wasn't exactly known for tolerance. One such nugget: avoid playing cards, or at least avoid *winning* at cards. According to Eisenstat, Greenberg told him: "I would suggest that you don't play, because you're liable to have some redneck who may have a comment when he loses."

"And that's all. We dropped it. I understood what he meant," said Eisenstat.[24]

While the Bengals were winning their games, Jake Powell—that Yankee who had barreled into Greenberg at first base in 1936—was beginning a ten-game suspension handed down by Commissioner Landis for his comments during that radio interview in which he used racial epithets about African Americans. But even as he meted out the punishment, Landis—who could never be mistaken for a great progressive when it came to race relations—told reporters that he "believed the 'remark was due more to carelessness than intent.'" [25]

Powell made an "apology tour," trying to make amends by visiting Harlem and buying drinks for the locals in various bars and clubs. But according to Steve Wulf on ESPN.com decades later, Powell did not suddenly have an epiphany and see the error of his ways: the Yankees ordered him to do so. "Powell visited various newspaper offices, businesses and bars, and the foray lasted a couple of days. While he did buy drinks for patrons, he was accompanied by a community leader named Hubert Julian. And his apologies were only half-hearted . . ."[26]

In fact, progressiveness across the spectrum was in short supply in general. The European refugee crisis continued to deteriorate. Headlines became more and more dire over the summer and moving into autumn. Many Americans became increasingly concerned about possible additional economic drains if the displaced were allowed to settle on US soil.

Politicians and observers in Europe tried to downplay the severity of the situation, unable or unwilling to believe anecdotal reports coming out of the regions. Figures varied wildly about the number of people imperiled.

Germany's immediate neighbors, still relatively unscathed by the encroaching Nazi stranglehold, shut down their borders. Some nations were sympathetic but either did not change their immigration policies or made them even more difficult. "The stress of refugees was now becoming a giant rushing current," wrote Michael R. Marrus in *The Unwanted: European Refugees in the Twentieth Century.*[27]

Greenberg's 35 home runs by July 29 had put him one ahead of Ruth. In a span of nine games, he had made up for his previous inconsistent play with nine home runs and 21 RBIs. But like the disclaimers on commercials for financial institutions, past performance is no guarantee of future results. Ruth hit 41 out by July 31, 1928, even better than in his record-setting year; by that point on the calendar in 1927, Ruth had "just" 34 home runs. But he hit only 13 more over the last two months of the 1928 season to finish at 54.

Hammerin' Hank's power flood was starting to attract attention outside the Detroit area. The Associated Press took the longview approach when it published their story, "Hank Greenberg's Home Spree Awaits Acid Test of September."

Along about this time every year, the Figure Filberts sharpen up their pencils, scribble numbers and confidently conclude that Joe Zilch or Luke Glotz has a chance to bust Babe Ruth's eleven-year-old record of sixty home runs in one season.

Baseball men will tell you those Filberts might just as well figure up their next year's income tax, because they'd come as close to the answer. For when you start monkeying with the Babe's all-time fence-busting high, the way to do that is with the final month of the season—that gaudy September when he parked seventeen long [for] the cash customers in thirty days—and work back.

The item goes back and forth about Greenberg's chances of catching or passing Ruth, concluding with a prediction: "[I]t's safe to say that if Hank can start September five homers in front of the Babe's pace, he has an even chance of wiping that mark off the books."[29]

Greenberg in July:

G	PA	AB	R	H	2B	3B	HR	RBI	BB	SO	BA	OBP	SLG
26	111	94	27	34	4	0	15	32	16	12	.362	.455	.883

Greenberg in 1938 (through July 30):

G	PA	AB	R	H	2B	3B	HR	RBI	BB	SO	BA	OBP	SLG
92	404	331	83	104	12	4	37	79	70	52	.314	.435	.710

Notes

1 "This Morning with Shirley Povich." *Washington Post*, July 27, 1938.

2 *Historical Statistics of the United States: Colonial Times to 1970, Part 1*. US Bureau of Census, 1975, pp. 166–76.

3 Hugh S. Fullerton Jr., "Attendance Record Set By 1938 Baseball." *Deseret News*, October 4, 1938.

4 Joe Falls, *The Detroit Tigers: An Illustrated History* (Walker and Company, 1989), pp. 69–70.

5 *The Detroit Tigers: An Illustrated History*, p. 73.

6 "Hank Decides Not to Play in All-Star Game." *Detroit Free Press*, July 2, 1938.

7 Wayne Stewart (edited and introduced), *The Gigantic Book of Baseball Quotations* (Skyhorse Publishing, 2007), pp. 314, 324.

8 Doc Holst, "Tiger Notes." *Detroit Free Press*, July 3, 1938.

9 In fact, from 1930–39, eight of the ten teams in first place on that date won the WS, with the only two teams being the '34 Cardinals (third) and '35 Tigers (second).

10   Ibid.

11   Charles P. Ward, "Greenberg Hits No. 24 and 25 as Tigers win, 4–0." *Detroit Free Press*, July 10, 1938.

12   *Detroit Free Press*, July 15, 1938.

13   Charles P. Ward, "Tiger Notes." *Detroit Free Press*, July 18, 1938.

14   Charles P. Ward, "Detroit to Get St. Louis Club! It's Old story." *Detroit Free Press*, July 19, 1938.

15   "Fans Go for Greenberg: Hank Goes for Wheaties!" *Detroit Free Press*, July 19, 1938.

16   "Ward to the Wise." *Detroit Free Press*, July 20, 1938.

17   "Missing Baron is Found; Says Nix to Minors." *Detroit Free Press*, July 22, 1938.

18   Charles P. Ward "York's Injury Revives Demand for Skullcap." *Detroit Free Press*, July 23, 1938.

19   Shirley Povich, "Greenberg's Home in 8th Inning Beats Nats, 6–5." *Washington Post*, July 27, 1938.

20   W. W. Edgar, "Nazi Fight Film Draws Protest of Louis Aides." *Detroit Free Press*, July 27, 1938.

21   Shirley Povich, "Greenberg Excels Ruth's Mark as Nats Lose, 9–4." *Washington Post*, July 28, 1938.

22   "This Morning with Shirley Povich." *Washington Post*, July 27, 1938.

23   *Hero of Heroes*, p. 158.

24   *Story of My Life*, p. 104.

25   "Powell is Banned by Judge Landis." *Detroit Free Press*, July 31, 1938.

26   Steve Wulf, "Bigot unwittingly sparked change." ESPN.com, February 22, 2014.

27 Michael R. Marrus, *The Unwanted: European Refugees in the Twentieth Century* (Oxford University Press, 1985).

28 *The Unwanted*, pp. 171–72.

29 *New York Herald Tribune*, July 31, 1938.

AUGUST

"[I]f I can keep pace with the record until September 7, I think I can do it."
> —Greenberg to a *New York Daily News* reporter in July.

"I've heard that question so much. . . that I even hear it now in my sleep. . . . Maybe I oughta get cards printed with 'Who knows?' on them."
> —Greenberg on the repetition of questions about his chances to catch Ruth.[1]

Bomb. Tater. Dinger. Salami. Blast. Poke. No-doubter. However many ways there are to say home run (*The Baseball Thesaurus* lists more than 100 variations), Greenberg had a lot of them by the end of July. So many that the press—and by extension, the fans—were starting to get excited that, hey, Hankus Pankus was in Babe Ruth territory! Practically each time Greenberg slammed one from here on out, the newspapers would find a way to make that comparison in their headlines.

After going 6-for-11 in the first three games of the series, Greenberg cooled down in the Tigers' final game against the A's, who remained in Detroit an extra day to make for Sunday's rain-out. Cochrane held court with the press while everyone waited to see whether this one would be called off as well. He praised Greenberg as one of the reasons for the team's recent hot streak and their overall resurgence. "He has quit pressing and is getting twice the distance with half the effort," said the proud manager.[2]

Trailing 4–0 after six innings in Monday's make-up game, Cochrane "remembered that Harry Eisenstat on Saturday had beaten the A's twice and that Hank Greenberg had delivered home runs in each game . . ." He brought in the reliever, who did his job by shutting out the A's in the ninth, "[b]ut the Greenberg part of the charm didn't work," wrote Doc Holst in his game recap. "Hank was the last man to bat in the ninth and he grounded out. But even had Hank delivered the *expected* home run, the Tigers would still have been behind, 4–2, as only Charlie Gehringer was on base at time." (emphasis added)[3]

So it had come to this; it was now "expected" that Greenberg would come through in the clutch in the most dramatic of styles.

Maybe he would have benefited from the experimental yellow baseball that made its debut on August 2 in the game between the St. Louis Cardinals and the host Brooklyn Dodgers. Reviews were mixed as the home team won the day, 6–2. Babe Ruth, coaching first for the Bums, said "I didn't even know it was yellow until somebody fouled one down there by me. The color don't make no difference." His teammate and nemesis Leo Durocher agreed. "When you hit the way I do . . . they can throw a red ball, a green ball, or a fancy dress ball even, and it doesn't make any difference. I can miss any and all kinds."[4]

Grantland Rice, one of the most venerated sportswriters of all time, took up the case between Greenberg and Ruth in his syndicated column "The Sportslight." Even in the 1930s, Rice was an avid member of the "things were better in my day" club.

"Down through the years, the home run records make interesting reading," he wrote. "They reflect the changes in the ball and a change, too, in batting styles." Rice brought up previous home run hitters: Philadelphia Phillies outfielder Gavvy Cravath, who led the NL in home runs six times in the 1910s and '20s, never hitting more than 24 in any season (and once winning the crown with a mere eight); Cy Williams, a four-time champ for the Chicago Cubs and Phillies; and George Kelly of the New York Giants, who led the NL with 23 in 1921 while Ruth was crushing 59 for the Yankees. What would it have been like, Rice wondered, if Nap Lajoie or "Wahoo" Sam Crawford or "Shoeless Joe" Jackson had had the opportunity to hit the lively ball like Greenberg? "This year the main prize for home run hitting seems to be rather securely in Greenberg's hands. He may not break the Babe's record but it is hard to see how any of his rivals can catch up with him."[5]

John Lardner—the son of Ring, another scribe in the Rice model—added his two cents in the parlance of the era in a syndicated article: "With Greenberg, you don't back up any throw at third base. You stand behind home plate with your cap off, scratching your head, and whistling six of eight bars of 'Am I Blue?' while the big kosher slugger charges around the bases like a herd of restless buffalo."

Like Rice and other writers of that generation, Lardner pointed out the advantage that Greenberg enjoyed, playing on a team whose home ballpark was more home-run friendly. "The Detroit park is nice and short," Lardner wrote, "a regular picnic ground for Greenberg."

And, again, like Rice and company, Lardner conceded the possibilities. "But Greenberg—well, I gotta hunch [sic] on him. He's liable to do it."[6]

As someone who followed Greenberg and the Tigers on a daily basis, the *Free Press'* Charles Ward was perhaps in a better position to offer a well-considered opinion. He stated the obvious that had yet to circulate outside the environs of Detroit.

> The biggest danger Greenberg faces in his assault on the Ruth record is pressure. When Ruth made his mark he was merely hitting straightaway and not trying for any record. If he made a home run on any certain day it was all right. If he didn't it was all right with him, too. He wasn't falling behind any schedule because he wasn't swinging according to schedule.
>
> With Greenberg it will be different. He will be continually reminded of the Ruthian pace. Every time he picks up a paper he will find that he is so many homers behind or ahead of Ruth's marks. This may cause him to press if he goes into a slump. The guy is high-strung and susceptible to pressure.[7]

C.M. Gibbs paraphrased the same concern in his "Gibberish" column in the August 4 edition of the *Baltimore Sun*, when he passed on the thoughts of the Yankees' All-Star catcher Bill Dickey. Greenberg had a good chance of breaking the record, according to the future Hall of Famer, but there was a stipulation:

"Dickey . . . qualifies that by saying that if Hank goes through two weeks without adding to his collection of 37 then he won't have much chance."[8]

And that is almost precisely what happened.

It was as if all this fresh attention was a whammy: Greenberg hit just one home run over his next 16 games, going homerless in nine straight from August 9th to 18th. During the first 18 days of the month the Tigers posted a record of 6–9–1, including a 3–3 standoff in the second game of a doubleheader with the Browns in St. Louis that was called on account of darkness. Perhaps all the Ruth talk *was* causing Greenberg to press just a bit. He batted just .267 from August 1st through the 18th, at one point going four straight games without a hit or a walk.

The latest skid proved to be the end of the line for Cochrane. On August 7, the Tigers fired their skipper, the news meriting full banner headlines on the front page of the *Free Press* just above "Jealous Husband Slain After Killing Wife's Bodyguard" and "Theft of Papers with Aid of Russian Secret Police Charged in U.A.W. Trial." The team was nestled in fifth place with a record of 47–51, 17 games behind the Yankees who had taken over first place from the Indians for good on July 13.

In his four-plus seasons with the Tigers, "Black Mike" won two pennants and a world's championship. Detroit finished in second place the other two seasons, so Cochrane deserved a good deal of credit and respect for his leadership, both in the dugout and behind the plate. He batted .313 with 11 home runs and 150 RBIs in 315 games, winning the MVP award in 1934 and twice being named an All-Star. But it was evident that he was having trouble controlling the team, part of which could be attributed to injuries. At the time of his firing, he was just thirty-five years old.

But as the old saying goes, managers are hired to be fired. Del Baker, whom sports pundits joked earlier in the season was the Edgar Bergman behind Greenberg's Charley McCarthy for signaling what pitches were coming, took up the reins. Greenberg gave him a welcoming gift with his 38th home run, a three-run shot in the first inning against Black Jack Wilson of the visiting Boston Red Sox in a 7–3 win before a crowd of 19,000.

The front page of the August 25 *Sporting News* carried the story of the Tigers' lackluster performance mingled with Greenberg's success. "The plain, if disappointing truth, seems to be that the Tigers simply did not have the strength to join seriously in the pennant fight," wrote Sam Greene. "Meanwhile the Tigers will play out the string, confident they are still good enough to earn the rewards of fourth position. They will have some consolation, too, in individual performances, the most satisfying of which is that of Henry Greenberg."[9]

Were the dog days of August starting to play a role as well? If having to deal with the hottest part of the season wasn't bad enough, the Tigers were forced to play three doubleheaders in the span of six days necessitated by early season rainouts. On August 13 against the St. Louis Browns, Greenberg clubbed two balls into the stands that curved foul at the last minute. While Doc Holst thought to mention these details in his "Tiger Notes" on August 14, there's no way of knowing how many similar misguided missiles Greenberg hit.

He was hitless in the two games against the Browns in St. Louis on August 14 and the next two against the visiting White Sox three days later. He did, however, pick up three ribbies on August 18.

In his "Calling 'Em Right" column of August 16, Bert Keane, sports editor for the *Hartford Courant*, wrote, "The month of

August is when a home run dispenser must click, Hank avers. In September shadows flit and frisk about the diamond to hamper you. Wild rookies fresh up from the minors keep you constantly in a cautious mood."

Keane also noted that it was impossible to please all of the people all of the time. "Yet when he fans occasionally, the boys in the stands boo him. Such are the vagaries of baseball."

Greenberg participated in a version of a "home run derby," prior to the game on August 14, with teammates York and Gehringer and three members of the Browns, each man allowed to choose his pitcher. York came away the winner, splitting the $150 pot with the Browns' Harlond Clift; each blasted a shot measured at 470 feet. Greenberg came in third. York spent the money on cigars and other small gifts for his teammates.

As the months went on, Germany continued to garner more attention in the American media. The *Free Press* ran two items on the front page, one marking a record-setting air trip between New York and Berlin by German flyers, the other perhaps a bit more ominous as the Reich was set to begin a series of war games along the French and Czech borders that was as much a show of force as anything else. The maneuvers were expected to last more than a month and drew anxious attention from a number of European nations, already nervous about Hitler's obsession for power and territory. The German minority living in the Sudetenland—the sections located in the northwest, northeast, and southwest borders of Czechoslovakia—wanted to live under control of their brethren, prompting fretful negotiations which ultimately resulted in a takeover similar to the *Anschluss* in March.

All this was of little concern to the average American. And what *they* might think was of even less importance to Hitler who believed the late entrance of the United States into World War I was proof of that nation's lethargy and insignificance. He held that the wrong side had won the "War Between the States," that the fact that so many nationalities and races lived together within one country was an indication of impurity and miscegenation, contrary to the concept of the cherished melting pot that was at the heart of American values.

At least that was the ideal situation, what America was supposed to be all about. But the truth was that there were a number of people within her borders who sided more with Hitler than Roosevelt. They banded into hate groups that almost seemed to battle each other for "top honors" in despicableness, most notably the well-established Ku Klux Klan and the relatively new Black Legion, which was based in Detroit. Then there was the German American Bund, an organization of Americans of German descent who supported the Nazi regime in their ancestral homeland. Despite their "competing" agendas, their philosophies were generally similar: hatred of foreigners, non-whites, and non-Christians. Their meetings drew thousands of people and raised concern from the targets of their animosity. The Bund and Black Legion eventually fell apart due to combination of backlash from decent Americans (not to mention legal prosecutions) and their own internal incompetence. But as we know, hate groups continue to spew their poison to this day.

Maybe that home run derby relaxed Greenberg a bit. He seemed to find his range in the August 19 doubleheader against the Browns, who had come to town for another visit.

The situation looked bad for the Tigers from the start, as they trailed 7–0 going into the fourth inning of the first game. They pushed two runs across in their half of the inning and loaded the bases after back-to-back walks, bringing Greenberg to the plate. He unloaded them with one swing, his second grand slam of the season, to bring Detroit within one run.

After the Tigers tied it up with a sacrifice fly by Dixie Walker in the seventh, Greenberg stepped up to the plate in the bottom of the ninth with the game tied and one out. Facing Fred Johnson, Hammerin' Hank parked one into the left-field grandstands for the walk-off win.

And he wasn't done for the day: His homer in the first inning of the nightcap with two men on fueled a five-run outburst that put the game out of reach in a 7–4 victory. It was the fifth straight win for the Tigers but, more importantly, it was Greenberg's 41st of the year, a personal best that put him a week ahead of the Babe; the Bambino didn't hit his 41st in 1927 until August 27.

Shirley Povich had always been one of those thoughtful writers who were not afraid to integrate the "outside world" with their assigned beat on occasion. In his *Washington Post* column of August 20, he ran a series of briefs items, concluding each one with a pithy wrap-up comment. He included Greenberg's busy day: "News item: 'Hank Greenberg hits three home runs, one with bases full, to beat Browns.' Comment—Ah, there Adolph."[10]

Greenberg was even making news outside US borders. The *Toronto Globe and Mail* ran a headshot of the ballplayer, extolling his exploits and putting him in Ruthian perspective. What's noteworthy about this tiny item was the headline: "Look Out, Babe!" This was the same catchphrase used thirty-six years later when another batter was challenging a record held by Babe Ruth: Hank Aaron.

As Birdie Tebbetts noted when comparing the struggles of Greenberg with those of Jackie Robinson, the same enmity applied to Aaron who received sack after sack of hate mail from those who did not want to see a member of a minority succeed in taking away such a significant record from a white man. Like Robinson, Aaron received numerous death threats as he approached Ruth's mark of 714 lifetime home runs, once thought unbreakable. And like Robinson, he could not hide.

Greenberg was homerless (and hitless) on August 20 when the Tigers won their sixth in a row to return to the .500 mark and move into fourth place, but he cracked No. 42 the next day in a 9–4 loss to Louis "Bobo" Newsom—dubbed "Loud Louie" by Ward.

Greenberg didn't do much against Newsom in his first three at-bats: he flied out in the first; hit a double play ball with the bases loaded that was botched in the third, with Greenberg earning credit for an RBI; and hit into a force play for the third out in the fourth. Patience. His measure of revenge came in the seventh.

Hank's homer was hit with twenty-four hours of pre-meditation. Before Saturday's game, Loud Louie met Big Hank in the runway leading to the clubhouse and crowed as how Hank was lucky he wasn't batting against him every day.

"You would be trying to set a record for loud foul balls instead of home runs if you were," he said.

"I'll bet you I hit a homer off you in this series," said Big Henry, bristling.

Loud Louie promised he would shake hands with him at home plate if he did.

When Greenberg's blast flew into the left field pavilion, "Loud Louie gazed sadly after it. True to his word, however, [he] walked to the plate and shook Greenberg's hand."[11] The RBI was his 100th of the year, the fourth time he had reached that milestone in five years.

After a day off on August 22, the Tigers traveled to the City of Brotherly Love for back-to-back doubleheaders, again the product of uncooperative weather earlier in the year. They split the series, sweeping the Tuesday games and dropping both on Wednesday.

Greenberg was hit in the arm by a Lynn Nelson pitch in the seventh in the opener of the August 23 doubleheader. He stayed in the game and scored on a Pete Fox single, but was replaced by Tebbetts in the bottom of the inning. It was the only playing time Greenberg missed all year, ruining an otherwise perfect attendance record.

"When Trainer Denny Carroll examined the arm in the club-house a short time later it was as swollen as a limb that had been worked upon by a swarm of serious-minded hornets," wrote Charles Ward. "But as soon as Greenberg learned it wasn't bro-ken, as it was feared, he said, 'Okay, Doc, you'll have to get that swelling down."[12] Greenberg knew he couldn't afford to miss any time if he was truly going to have a chance at catching the Babe.

And he kept to his word in the second game of the day, hitting his 43rd home run to lead off the sixth inning to give his team a 5–2 lead. He also added an RBI double in the ninth en route to an 8–3 win.

Germany wasn't the only foreign power meriting attention in the media. Japan was also in the mix, as the *Free Press* reported in a story with the headline "Jap Warplanes Down Airliner; 14 Feared Lost." According to the AP report, the plane—"Chinese-American owned"—was carrying "two women, a baby, a small child, and 11 men as passengers and a four-man crew" when it was shot down by machine gun fire on the South China coast.[13]

Back in Europe, Great Britain made a fateful decision when it pledged to enter the fray if the Nazis attacked Czechoslovakia, joining the Soviet Union in support of the embattled nation. In a move similar to the *Anschluss*, Germany asked England and France to pressure the Czech government to grant autonomy to Germans living in the Sudetenland. But Great Britain warned they were prepared to take action if Germany sought to use force; the government announced the mobilization of the Royal Navy in response to Nazi military exercises. That was basically an empty gesture, more for show than anything else. In private, however, Prime Minister Neville Chamberlin was preparing to sign a non-aggression pact with Germany.

From Philly it was down to DC for a three-game set. The teams split the first two and the Tigers almost gave away the finale when the Senators scored two in the bottom of the ninth, though they still came up short in a 12–11 decision. Greenberg's 44th home run, which led off a five-run fourth inning, went deep into the center-field stands and put him four days ahead of Ruth's pace. The seesaw Tigers were back at the .500 mark at 59–59, but fell back into fifth place.

Number 45 came the next day in a 10-inning, 4–3 win over the Red Sox at Fenway Park. His solo shot in the seventh went over the left-field wall, which was not yet colloquially known as the "Green Monster." He was now nine days ahead of Ruth.

Greenberg ended the month with 46 home runs, the most recent coming on August 31 in a 12–6 win over the Yankees in the Bronx. The ball went into the left-field stands with the bases empty and two out in the second inning, accounting for one of his three RBIs for the afternoon and 113 on the season. Ruth, by contrast, hit his 46th in his 128th game. Greenberg was five games ahead of the pace.

Regardless of the increased frequency of the home runs, Greenberg was trying to keep a low profile, hedging his bets. In an August 26 interview, he told reporters he considered his chances to catch Ruth "slim."

"'Every time I come to bat I'm trying to hit a homer,' he said. 'The fans want them. The result is my batting average has slipped to about .299.'" (In fact, he finished the month at .306.) He also noted another factor:

"'[T]hey're giving me more intentional passes than ever, just like they did Ruth. And I guess they're dusting me off a little bit, too. I've been hit by pitched balls twice in the last couple of games.'" Again, this was incorrect; the last time he had been plunked was in the first game of the August 23 doubleheader. And only one of the 21 free passes he received that month were classified as intentional, and since statistics for that category are incomplete, that part of his statement is similarly difficult to confirm.

One would hate to think Greenberg was making excuses for the possibility of falling short of the target.

> "But here's where I'm handicapped. We're going into September, and that's usually bad weather for homers. There's the wind, which dulls the hitting. And, finally, the pitchers gain an advantage because shadows fall over the playing field earlier, making it tougher on the batters."

At that point, Greenberg had 36 games left. Twenty-six of those would be played at his home field with the ten road games in New York, Chicago, St. Louis, and Cleveland.

When reporters pointed out that Ruth hit his last 17 home runs in September in his record-setting season, Greenberg was graciously eloquent:

> "Yeah," said Hank, "the Babe was a wonder slugger. My hat's still off to him. But I'm going to keep knocking baseballs on wood until my 36 games are up—and maybe Ruth's number."[14]

Perhaps he was being a bit guarded because he had been down this road before. In his memoirs, he recalled an interview with the *New York Evening Post* in which he said he had 30 homers by the end of July in 1935, but hit just six more during the final months of the campaign. In actuality the figures were 28 and eight respectively, which doesn't sound quite as sexy as 30. But his point was made: I'm not going to count my chickens.

Ruth's former Yankee mates such as Lou Gehrig, Red Ruffing, and manager Joe McCarthy all offered varying degrees of conviction that Greenberg had a good chance to at least tie the record. But the Tiger still demurred. "I'll begin to give it serious thought if I finish August with 50 homers," he said. "If I don't, I'm cooked."[15]

Greenberg once said, "The only way you can get along with newspapermen is to say something one minute and something different the next." Maybe that explains why he would present a different attitude from one day to the next. With 33 games remaining, he told Bill McCullough of the *Brooklyn Eagle* that his target for the season had been 40, a number he had thrown out in spring training. According to that goal, "Any homers I hit now are nothing but gravy. . . . Sure I'd like to tie or bust the Babe's mark. But I'm not straining myself. If I don't I have nothing to lose. The way things shape up now, I ought to lead both leagues in hitting homers. That's an honor just in itself."[16]

Greenberg in August:

G	PA	AB	R	H	2B	3B	HR	RBI	BB	SO	BA	OBP	SLG
31	140	116	26	33	6	0	9	34	21	20	.284	.403	.569

Greenberg in 1938 (through August 31):

G	PA	AB	R	H	2B	3B	HR	RBI	BB	SO	BA	OBP	SLG
123	544	447	109	137	18	4	46	113	91	72	.306	.427	.673

Notes

1   *Story of My Life*, p. 109.
2   Charles P. Ward, "Lawson faces Macks Today." *Detroit Free Press*, August 1, 1938.
3   Doc Holst, "A's End Tiger Streak—Gill to Face Yanks Today." *Detroit Free Press*, August 2, 1938.
4   Henry McLemore, "Yellow Ball Trial Ended With 'Hung Jury.'" *St. Louis Star and Times*, August 3, 1938.
5   Grantland Rice, "The Sportlight . . . Greenberg and the Babe." *Detroit Free Press,* August 3, 1938.
6   John Lardner, "Hank Makes Real Threat on '60' Mark." *Hartford Courant*, August 3, 1938.
7   Charles P. Ward, "Ward to the Wise." *Detroit Free Press*, August 4, 1938.
8   C. M. Gibbs, "Gibberish." *Baltimore Sun*, August 4, 1938.
9   Sam Greene, "Greenberg Keeps Ahead of Pace of Ruth in Record Homer Year." *The Sporting News*, August 25, 1938.
10 Shirley Povich, "This Morning." *Washington Post*, August 20, 1938.
11 Charles P. Ward, "Newsom Snaps Tigers' Winning Streak; Hank Hits No. 42." *Detroit Free Press*, August 22, 1938.
12 Charles P. Ward, "Greenberg Hits No. 43 as Tigers Trounce A's Twice." *Detroit Free Press*, August 24, 1938.
13 *Detroit Free Press*, August 25, 1938.
14 "Hank Greenberg Sees Slim Chance of Breaking Ruth's Homer Record." *Christian Science Monitor*, August 31, 1938.
15 *Story of My Life*, p. 108.
16 Bill McCullough, "Homers He Hits Now Just Gravy, Says Greenberg—Using No Napkin." *Daily Eagle*, August 31, 1938.

SEPTEMBER–OCTOBER

"I'm sorry, Hank. But this is as far as I can go."
"That's all right, George. This is as far as I can go, too."
—Exchange between home plate umpire George
Moriarty and Hank Greenberg as the last game of the
season against the Indians in Cleveland was called
after seven innings on account of darkness.[1]

"That's all right. I don't think I could have eaten 61."
—Greenberg on the amount of pieces of gefilte
fish his mother promised to make if he broke
Ruth's home run record.

Roger Maris was a quiet, down-to-earth kind of guy. Born and raised in Fargo, North Dakota, he didn't take to the clamor of living in New York City as did his best friend, Mickey Mantle, who hailed from the small coalmining town of Commerce, Oklahoma.

Maris did not enjoy the spotlight, so when it was his turn to challenge Ruth's single-season home run mark in 1961, being the center of all that scrutiny was not something he relished. Reporters wouldn't leave him alone, pestering him the with same questions day after day, especially as the end of the season approached.

For much of 1961, the "M&M Boys" were both chasing Ruth. Mantle was a favorite of the press, always happy to share a drink and a joke. He was their shining boy. Maris, on the other hand, was more private and, well . . . dull, at least to the fellows who covered the team. Perhaps if Mantle hadn't missed nine games due to injury and stayed closer in the home run race—he finished with 54, the second-highest of his career—they would have focused on Maris less.

As the number of home runs increased and he began to catch up to Ruth, the suits in baseball's headquarters started to get nervous. Who was this pissant to challenge the mighty Babe? Maris wasn't fit to carry Ruth's jock, they said behind closed doors.

Ford Frick, then the commissioner of baseball but previously a sports journalist and the ghostwriter for *Babe Ruth's Own Book of Baseball,* just couldn't see it. There had to be some way to differentiate what his pal did in 154 games with what Maris might accomplish given the benefit of the additional eight chances now that the American League had expanded to ten teams beginning in 1961. (In addition, there was some thought Maris was given a leg up because the quality of pitching was watered down since those hurlers on the two new ball clubs might otherwise not have had a chance to be in the major leagues.)

On July 26, Maris had 40 home runs, Mantle 38. Frick announced in a press conference, "Babe Ruth's mark of 60 home runs, made in a schedule of 154 games in 1927, cannot be broken unless some batter hits 61 or more within his club's first 154 games."[2]

According to legend, Frick suggested some typographical mark be attached to the numeral should Maris or someone else reach that magical mark. The infamous asterisk was never actually employed, but is it any surprise that all this tumult caused Maris's hair to fall out?

He tied Ruth on September 26 in a 3–2 win over the visiting Baltimore Orioles. It took him another five games to set the new record. Number 61 came off Tracy Stallard on October 1, the final day of the season, to give the Yankees a 1–0 win over the Red Sox.

Hank Greenberg was also linked at the hip to Babe Ruth as the 1938 season drew to a close. The Yankees clinched the AL pennant on September 18, giving way for "the chase" to dominate headlines. Over in the National League, the Cubs kept the excitement going until the last couple of days. Player-manager Gabby Hartnett provided one of the most memorable moments in major league history when his "homer in the gloamin'"—the encroaching darkness—in the bottom of the ninth inning beat the Pittsburgh Pirates 6–5 on September 28 to help secure the pennant.

If it was any comfort to him, Hammerin' Hank *only* had to deal with print media (and a smidgen of radio) while Maris had the added pressure of the television cameras which presented even more of an intrusion by sticking a metaphorical nose in his business.

Greenberg, though, also faced a constant repetition of questions: How do you feel? What's your strategy? What do you think about the way the opposition is pitching you? What did you have for breakfast? (Wheaties, of course!)

"Hankus-Pankus Greenberg has taken to ducking when he sees them coming," wrote John Lardner, "meaning the fellows with paper and pencils in their pockets who ask him whether his intentions toward Babe Ruth's home run record are honorable or dishonorable?"

How many ways can you answer the same question? Lardner took objection to Greenberg's pat response, that the record was a constant thought for him, "[w]hich is like saying that rain is wet," he wisecracked.[3]

Jewish publications, which understandably had more serious issues to cover at the time, took to offering primers to their readers who might not have followed sports heretofore, attempting to explain the basics of the game—including what a home run was. It was reminiscent of an editorial published in 1903 in the *Jewish Daily Forward*, a popular Yiddish newspaper in which a father had written to ask if it was all right to allow young Jewish boys to take up baseball.

"Let your boys play . . . and even become outstanding players as long as it doesn't interfere with their studies and doesn't put them in bad company," answered *Forward* editor Abraham Cahan. He extolled the virtues of the game as developing hand-eye coordination and giving the youngsters a chance to get out in the fresh air. But there was another aspect that was perhaps more important: acceptance.

"Let's not raise our children to be foreigners in their own country," Cahan urged. "An American who isn't agile and strong in hands, feet and his entire body is not an American. . . . Raise your children as educated and thoughtful; as people filled with the true heritage of humanity and fellowship for which they are ready to fight. They should also be healthy and agile youth who shouldn't feel inferior to others."

Cahan didn't have such nice things to say about another sport that was gaining in popularity. "Football, the 'aristocratic' sport of the colleges, now there is a wild game. You fight with each other like Indians and often one is left with a broken foot or hand or gets wounded. But there is no danger in baseball," he wrote.[4]

Lots of Jews took his advice to heart. By the time Greenberg was establishing himself as a star some thirty years later, a generation had grown up with the game and, in a role reversal, these kids were teaching their parents about the nuances of baseball, pointing to the Hebrew Hammer as an example of what they could aspire to be.

"For the next few weeks, the incidents in Palestine, in Germany, in Czechoslovakia, take a back seat," the *Boston Jewish Advocate* printed on its op-ed page. "They are not important. We have had pogroms before; we have had wars before; we have had trouble with the Arabs before. But never before have we had a Jewish home-run king." The writer obviously was unaware of Lipman Pike, the New York-born son of Dutch Jews, who played in the late nineteenth century and led the majors—at least that era's version of the majors—in home runs *four* times, never hitting more than seven in any season.

At a time when anti-Semitism in the United States was perhaps at its strongest point, the *Advocate* noted how it was good for the Jews to have someone like Greenberg serving as standard-bearer.

"Greenberg is a great ball player, and in his way something else," the publication proclaimed. "He is another form of good-will emissary for the Jewish people in America. He doesn't make speeches; he doesn't give money to non-Jewish causes; he doesn't sponsor brotherhood meetings. He simply hits home runs, and the crowd goes wild."[5]

The non-sports news of the world grew increasing dire during the final weeks of the season. The headlines of the September 3 *Free Press* screamed "WPA Job Grab Charged" atop "Kidnapped Ranch Woman Is Feared Slain." Surprisingly, of lesser note: "Hitler Sits Alone in Villa to Decide Europe's Fate."

The following day Hitler made his decision, according to the *Free Press* which exclaimed in three bold lines: "Germany Moves 50,000 troops into New Line of Forts on Rhine and Clamps French Border Shut."

But with the Labor Day holiday in full swing, it's questionable how many readers paid that much attention. More aligned with American concerns was "New Deal Efforts to Spread Wealth Fail, Survey Shows," announcing the shocking news that more than 40 percent of families in the country were earning less than $1,000 a year.

That wasn't the case for major leaguers, however, and if they wanted to increase their earning potential, this was the time to show the front office their value to the team.

The Tigers were not going to finish any higher than fourth place, if that well. After their holiday doubleheader against the Browns, they were 65–62, 23 games behind the Yankees, 9.5 behind the second-place Red Sox, and 8.5 back of the third-place Indians.

Including their last two games in August as part of their series at Yankee Stadium, Greenberg might have thought he had at least a psychological advantage: 22 of the Tigers' last 36 games were held at Briggs Stadium, including 20 straight from September 11 to the 29th. As of the end of August, 25 of his 46 home runs had come at home.

Once the calendar turned the page, the advantage Greenberg had enjoyed in recent months vanished: he went eight straight games without a home run to start the final push. Over that stretch—in which the Tigers went 4–4—their cleanup hitter drove in just two runs, again failing in his responsibilities as the slugger in the middle of the lineup. "When there are men on the bases it is your job to get them in," he often said in one form or another.[6] For those eight games, *he* was one of those men on base: two doubles, three singles . . . and 11 walks, including eight over the course of two contests.

This is where the arguments about a "conspiracy" began to get a bit more attention, with accusations that opponents were pitching around Greenberg over those last several weeks, not wanting to give the Jew a chance to break Ruth's record. According to Billy Rogell in Greenberg's memoirs, "'[T]hey'd walk Hank. I guess they just didn't want him to beat Babe Ruth's record. Because he was a Jew? Rogell was asked. 'I don't think just because he was Jewish, but that had a lot to do with it,' he said."[7]

But Harry Eisenstat thought otherwise. "Frankly, I think the pitchers were just trying to get him out and they were trying to be too fine. They walked him and he hit a few good balls, but like on that last day, the ball didn't carry. And I don't think they were deliberately walking him."[8] Maybe that was an honest

129

assessment, or maybe it was the pitcher recalling some advice Greenberg had given him when he joined the team.

> Hank told me, "Don't ever use the term, 'because you're Jewish,' if you don't do well. You do well in playing ball, you'll never hear it come up. But if you don't do well, other people will use it as an excuse." Hank said, "'It should be more of an incentive to be successful.'"

I guess it's all in the way you analyze the data. Greenberg was the only batter walked on September 3 by two White Sox pitchers in an 11–4 win. The next game he was the recipient of two free passes from Johnny Rigney (who also walked two other Tigers) in a 2–1 loss. Lefty Mills walked him three more times in the Tigers' 3–2 loss in the first game of a September 5 doubleheader against the Browns in St. Louis. In each of those games, Greenberg had two or fewer official turns at bat.

Greenberg fell a game behind Ruth's pace when he failed to homer off the Indians' wunderkind Bob Feller in a 6–0 loss on September 6 in Detroit. He hit one ball that might have been out in other ballparks, but being in his usually comfortable surroundings at Briggs didn't help this time: it missed going over the fence by a couple of feet. To add insult to injury, the ball took a fortuitous bounce off the wall to the Indians' outfielder who threw out Greenberg as he tried to stretch a single into a double.

Throughout the month he was under the sportswriters' microscopes. Although each ball hit out of the park was subject to a bit of embellishment and purple prose here and there, so too was each shortfall. "This one just missed." "That one would have been out in (fill-in-the-blank)." "Hank hit into some bad luck." The variations seemed infinite.

If he found the pressure getting to be too much, he could always pack it in and apply for a job as an inconspicuous US customs inspector; on the same page that carried the game story, the *Cleveland Plain Dealer* ran an advertisement for a correspondence course that claimed one could earn $2,100 in their first year on the job.

Greenberg failed to get a homer in the next two games as well, although he did drive in what proved to be a game-winning double in a 4–1 decision over the Indians to break Cleveland's nine-game winning streak. And, after all, that was what he always said gave him the most satisfaction. In that 1980 interview for the American Jewish oral history project, Greenberg repeated his goal: to average an RBI per game. The home runs were nice, of course—they gave a charge to the fans—but Greenberg knew runs came across the plate in a variety of fashions.

Greenberg hit his 47th on September 9 against the Indians' Ken Jungels in Cleveland as part of an 11–5 romp. But with the Yankees beating the Washington Senators that day as well (Gehrig appeared in his 2,100th consecutive game for the Bombers), it meant the Tigers were officially eliminated from the pennant race, even if that had pretty much been a foregone conclusion for months.

Newspapers around the nation took up the Ruth-Greenberg story. The *Daily Boston Globe* kept track of Greenberg's progress with a little capsule comparing the two sluggers, a sort of almanac deconstructing how he fared in each at-bat and noting how many round-trippers Greenberg and Ruth had by a given date.

Greenberg didn't have to wait long to add to his total, cranking out two more in a 10–1 mauling of the White Sox in the first game of a September 11 doubleheader.

He hit the half-century mark the next day in his 135th game, a solo shot into the left-field bleachers with two outs in the third inning in a 4–1 win to sweep the series against Chicago.

A headline over the September 13 *Washington Post* announced that Greenberg had hit his 50th, becoming just the third player to reach that lofty target. (That story shared space with the news that Gil Hunt, a local product, had defeated Bobby Riggs—yes, *that* Bobby Riggs—at the US Tennis Open in Forest Hills.)

The solo missile went into the upper deck of Briggs' left field stands in a 4–3 win over the visiting White Sox, the only game on the schedule for September 12. It put Greenberg four games ahead of the Babe's pace with 20 still left to play. "[He] must hit better than one home run every two games to better the mark," the Associated Press reported.

Charles Ward optimistically noted, "If he hits homers Thursday and Friday in the first and second game of a three-game series against the Yankees he will go ahead of the Ruth mark, for they will give him a total of 54 for the season and Ruth did not hit No. 54 in 1927 until the hundred and forty-third game"[9] (Friday would mark the Tigers' 139th game).

As Greenberg was piling up the home runs, sports columnists outside the Detroit area sought to catch their readers up on the significance of this historic sporting event, offering the full backstory, sometimes including Greenberg's religion in order to ramp up the "fish-out-of-water" or, perhaps more liturgically, "stranger in a strange land" angle. Referring to Ruth and his record-setting accomplishment in his September 14 "Down in Front" column,

Richards Vidmer wrote: "Ten years ago they were saying, with eyes of wonder and firm conviction, that there would never be another. . . . But now, ten years later, Hank Greenberg, a boy from the Bronx, stands within reach of even the greatest mark of the great Babe. He is within striking distance of the record no one expected to be even approached, much less passed."

Vidmer went on to emphasize the Babe's outsized personality that made him a living legend, regardless of statistics and comparisons between him and this young pretender to the home run crown.

"In the remaining days of the season, Hank Greenberg, a quiet, polite and splendid young fellow may hit 10 more home runs and equal Ruth's record. But even if he does, they were still right ten years ago when they said there never would be another Babe."[10] This was a sentiment that Greenberg himself would repeat often, perhaps out of a combination of humility and reverence for Ruth's place in the baseball firmament.

Even when Greenberg only hit long fly balls, sportswriters analyzed their quality. He was 0-for-3 in a 6–4 win against the visiting Yankees on September 15, but as Peter Ward wrote in his "Tiger Notes" for the game: "Greenberg's fly ball to center in the fifth might have been a homer if the wind had been coming from another direction. It traveled 400 feet before DiMaggio grabbed the ball."[11] This just shows how far Greenberg had come: no one would have ever thought to keep track of his long fly outs earlier in the season.

Vidmer—that wet blanket—deflated the good feelings and excitement of the Greenberg situation when he wrote, "Even if

[he] succeeds in tying or even breaking the record . . . it seems to me the annual award for the most valuable player in the league should go to someone else." He had a point, discouraging as it might be for Greenberg's fans to hear. Even though the Tigers had enjoyed a revival, winning 37 of 58 games since Del Baker took over in August, the Tigers had spent most of 1938 in a deep hole and struggled to finish with a little bit of self-respect.

While acknowledging that matching or setting a new home run record would undoubtedly stand out as a major accomplishment, Vidmer compared it to Johnny Vander Meer's back-to-back no-hitters that season which "didn't add any more to the success of the Reds than a couple of 15–9 games." Likewise, he wrote, "Greenberg's amazing home run hitting hasn't helped the Tigers very far along the way, as you will notice by a glance at the standings of the club."[12]

It could simply have been that many of the older sportswriters just appreciated and even loved Babe Ruth. Yes, he was also a symbol of the new age of the national pastime, bringing the game back from the precipice following the "Black Sox" scandal. The Big Bam's boyish personality and heretofore unheard-of power made the game fun again, ushering in a new type of hero: the power hitter. But more important to the writers was that he was a constant source of material, pulling off some crazy stunt on a regular basis. Sure, some of it was a bit too salacious to report in their papers (as opposed to today's "no holds barred" instant media). The boys at the sports desks were just protecting their interests. They wanted to stay on the good side of the ballclubs, which often provided transportation and meals in exchange for presenting a generally positive outlook.

The Babe waffled as he weighed in on Greenberg's chances: "The strain is too great. The boys are forever reminded about that record and it is bound to tell on them. It's telling on [him] now. I don't think he'll be able to make it now." But he contradicted himself to Jimmy Cannon of the *New York Daily News*, calling Greenberg "a great kid" and saying "[L]ate September is not as tough as you think to hit 60. Doubleheaders pile up and scores are high. Pitchers are worn out from a long summer's campaign. Hank'll be all right if they don't walk him too much. You can't hit a home run on pitchouts."[13] Ruth must have forgotten that twinbills in the fall also meant earlier sunsets and more shadows.

Routine things that never seemed to bother Greenberg before became an issue. In his day, photographers were actually allowed to shoot while stationed in foul territory. The bigger the occasion, the more shutterbugs. "[They] crowded the field when Hank batted, at the edge of his peripheral vision, their noisy cameras snapping away" wrote John Rosengren in *Hank Greenberg: The Heroes of Heroes*. "He didn't want to complain about the attention . . . but they were a distraction."[14]

An item in the September 16 *Brooklyn Eagle* announced "Yankees Put Hex on Hank." In the long run it was prescient, but not at that moment as the Tigers hosted the New Yorkers. An unidentified Bronx Bomber said, "The way Hank has been going in the last two weeks it appears as though the pressure is becoming too much for him. The big fellow is trying too hard and when you are in there with a bat in your hand that way you are not hitting naturally."

And it was true. Greenberg went 0-for-3 with a walk in the first game of the series. The next two days, however, provided different outcomes.

Hank hit number 51 in a 6–4 loss on the 16th. The *Free Press* ran a photo of Greenberg with the number "51" in a starburst with the title "Nine to Tie, Ten to Crack Ruth's Record." Ward wasn't overly lavish with his depiction of the latest sock. "As Greenberg's homers go, Hank's contribution yesterday was not much. It was a high fly that barely cleared the wall as George Selkirk leaped and pawed at it like a cat chasing a butterfly."[15] That didn't matter much to Lefty Gomez, the pitcher who gave up the long ball. The year before he had told Joe DiMaggio, "Roomie, you keep playing Greenberg shallow and you're going to make them forget [me]," after Greenberg hit an RBI triple over the sophomore outfielder's head. Gomez had wanted the Yankee Clipper to play deeper, but the overly-confident DiMaggio told him not to worry, that he was so talented he was going to make everyone forget about Tris Speaker, an outstanding defensive artist who was famous for playing shallow.[16]

The Yankees probably wished they hadn't poked the Tiger in that *Eagle* story. Didn't they know he had more home runs against them than any other club in the AL? Perhaps motivated by the jibe, he added his 52nd and 53rd blasts on the 17th to lead Detroit to a 7–3 victory and salvage the series. First he put his team on the board with a two-run homer in the bottom of the first and later gave them the winning margin with a three-run bomb in the fifth. It was the ninth time Greenberg had clubbed a pair in a game, one shy of the record set by Foxx in 1932. More importantly, they also put him ahead of Ruth's pace once again. *The New York Times* reported that he "was so eager to get another crack at [Yankees pitcher Monte] Pearson in the fourth that he started off the field with only two Yankees expunged."

They also noted that Greenberg broke his "home-run bat" in the seventh after knocking his fourth straight hit of the afternoon.[17] Batters are notoriously finicky about the tools of their profession, whether gloves or bats. The Louisville Slugger Museum in Kentucky features an order form submitted by Greenberg with exacting details as per length, weight, handle width, and other dimensions. As the season drags on and the batters get more fatigued, it's not unusual for a player to switch to something a bit lighter so he can get around on the ball faster.

Just as with Maris twenty-three years later, there were those who protested that should Greenberg match or exceed Ruth, there should be some sort of caveat. Why? With the exception of an abbreviated 1918 and 1919 due to World War I and it's aftermath, all teams prior to 1961 played a 154-game schedule. Ah, but wait. The naysayers pointed out that Ruth had played in just 151 of the Yankees' 154 games (number 60 came in their last game of the year). So for everything to be on the up-and-up, if Greenberg reached 60 or 61, it should be considered a tied or new record only if he made it in the same number of games as Ruth.

But why should Greenberg be penalized? No other record carried such a qualifier. Was it his fault if he was his team's "Iron Man," appearing in every scheduled game (plus that one tie) while Ruth had missed three? Nevertheless, there were those newspapermen who complained about the "advantage" Greenberg had because of those extra opportunities. If you want to be really fair about it, it might be more accurate to compare their plate appearances. A look at the statistics shows that Greenberg actually had ten fewer total trips to the plate in 1938—681—than Ruth did in 1927—691. Greenberg had 556 official at-bats to Ruth's 540. The big difference: Ruth walked 18 more times than Greenberg, 137 to 119.

In his "Tiger Notes" following the game, Charles Ward picked up on these chauvinistic squabbles:

> "If Hank Greenberg breaks the home run record of Babe Ruth he will have to do so despite the best efforts of some of Ruth's partisans from the "Big Boig." When Hank tied the Ruth record yesterday, these press box Darrows argued that he had done no such thing.
>
> "You guys had a tie game in there," they argued, "so this is really your one hundred and fortieth instead of your hundred and thirty-ninth game."[18]

Greenberg failed to homer in an 8–1 win over the Senators on September 18, the day the Yankees sewed up another pennant (even as they lost a doubleheader to the Browns). Despite the lopsided win, the *Free Press* headline cried "Hank's Bat Is Silent as Bridges Beats Nats." They also ran a box describing "What Hank Did," plate appearance-by-plate appearance. Similarly, the next day the *Free Press* proclaimed "Kennedy Fails on 13th as Hank Gets One Hit" in the Tigers' 12–2 loss.

In his September 20 "Star Sports Shots" in the *Chicago Heights Star*, a sportswriter with the byline "Meidell" added this little item at the end of his brief column about the forthcoming World Series: "Note to State Department, U.S.: If the Nazis don't behave, send Hank Greenberg over there to hit 'em with a ball bat."

That day's game against the visiting Philadelphia A's was cancelled due to inclement weather, so another one of those dreaded late-season doubleheaders was in order on September 21. Evidently the dreaded cool and damp weather didn't bother Greenberg too much: he hit his 54th home run—putting him two games ahead of Ruth's pace—in the first inning of the first game. In his second at-bat, he hit the ball so hard that third baseman Billy Werber had to be removed from the game and taken to a nearby hospital to see if the thumb on his glove hand was broken. In Greenberg's third trip to the plate, he sent a rocket to center, some 420 feet away, only to have Wally Moses flag it down. Had the same ball been pulled to left, it would have been home run number 55. Even so, he finished the game with six RBIs, with three coming on his first-inning blast.

Greenberg was hitless in the second game, a 3–0 Tigers win that was called after five innings because of darkness. Since he had three at-bats in that short span, it's a given he would have had at least one more opportunity had the game lasted a full nine innings.

Another foul day on September 22 cancelled *another* game, this one with the incoming Indians whom the Tigers were desperately trying to overtake for a third-place finish, a major accomplishment given how badly they had played earlier in the season. And that meant *another* doubleheader, with the distinct possibility that the nightcap would again not be played to completion, depriving Greenberg of irreplaceable at-bats.

He had a single in four at-bats in the opener, an 8–1 defeat. But almost as expected, the nightcap was called after seven innings. Greenberg made the most of his three official at bats (plus a walk), going 3-for-3 with two more home runs, bringing his total to 56 and establishing a record for most two-homer games in a season, breaking the mark of nine set by Foxx set earlier in the season and which had, in turn, supplanted Ruth's record of eight games set in 1927 and tied by Hack Wilson three years later.

Both of Greenberg's blasts came off Earl Whitehill. "[T]he latter caused [the pitcher] to kick the back of the mound in disgust with himself, for he and Hank have been something less than pals since away back in Earl's Tiger days."[19] Ward devoted his September 25 column to explaining the bad blood between the two.

When Greenberg reported to spring training in 1930, Whitehill was already an established player who felt his seniority earned him the right to hang around first base during practices rather than shagging flies in the outfield or doing any real conditioning. The rookie culture of the era dictated there was little Greenberg could do but swallow his pride and accede to custom. But when it came to hitting against Whitehill in batting practice or scrimmages, he took extra delight in bearing down and getting a hit.

Greenberg never forgot what he considered disrespectful treatment. According to Ward, however, "Whitehill apparently hasn't taken the feud as seriously." Still, "he never lets Hank forget that he likes to strike him out."[20]

Whitehill offered another one of those fun trivia notes offered by the newspapers during the home run race, serving as a link between Greenberg and Ruth: He was one of two pitchers who had surrendered home runs to both sluggers in their record seasons. The other was Ted Lyons, who pitched his entire career for the Chicago White Sox from 1923–45, minus a three-year gap during World War Two.

Reprising his pidgin English-speaking fans from his column on pitcher Al Milnar earlier in the season, the *Cleveland Plain*

Dealer's James Doyle sought to prove that even foreigners knew the importance of Babe Ruth.

> "What's 'bout dees beeg guy, Hank Greenberk?" said Mr. Ivan Offulitch. "You're t'eenk he's can beat babe Ruth for lots home runs?"
>
> "Babe Ruth wuss h'all by h'own self," replied Mr. Stanislaus Totaloss. "Hank Greenberk iss purry goot younk one but nobody's can beat Babe Ruth."[21]

Shortly after Greenberg hit his latest home runs, Sam Greene wrote of how one successful player can act as a salve if his team has been disappointing. With Detroit assured of no worse than a fourth-place finish, attention had turned almost exclusively to Greenberg's quest. Tiger fans "did not sag" after a double-header loss ruled out any chance at finishing third, he said in his September 29 article in *The Sporting News.* "Leaving the park, they were talking not of the double defeat, but of Greenberg's two drives into the left field stands.

"The important thing of the day—any day—is not that Detroit won or lost, but whether 'Hank hit another one.'" Or, to put it in a language many of his Jewish followers would understand, *Vos hot Greenberg geton haynt?* (What did Greenberg do today?)

Their hero went homerless on Saturday, September 24 ("Hank Shut Out as Goal Fades"), in a 7–6 win in which the Tigers scored six times in the bottom of the seventh to cap another improbable comeback. It was more of the same the next day:

"Greenberg Bat is Silent Again" in another Detroit win, the title above the box score pleading "C'mon, Hank."[22]

"Greenberg's failure was not entirely his fault," Ward wrote following the game, "for the Indians were very wary about pitching to the big bomber from the Bronx. Twice he was walked by Mel Harder, the first time on four pitches. It was obvious that the Indian hurlers were determined to give big Henry nothing good to hit."[23] So was this indeed a case of anti-Semitism, as more than a few at the time and since have theorized? Or was it just the opposition trying to win the game by not letting the Tigers' best hitter beat them, especially after he had hit two home runs just the day before?

Trade rumors in baseball have been a major enjoyment of fans since the first game was played in Hoboken, New Jersey, in 1846. And there's little they find more exciting than when the discussion involves marquee stars, as was the case with the late-season speculations that Greenberg and DiMaggio would swap addresses.

"New York is more or less agog over a report that the Yankees may get the Tigers' Hank Greenberg," according to the September 24 "Ward to the Wise." In this scenario, Big Henry would go back to the Bronx in exchange for DiMaggio and take the place of Lou Gehrig at first base. "What Lou would do the yarn sayeth not."

The deal made sense for a number of reasons, wrote Ward. "Greenberg, being Jewish, would prove an attraction to a great part of New York's population. The fact that Hank's home is in the vicinity of Yankee Stadium also is regarded as a point in favor of the deal."

"A transfer of DiMaggio and Greenberg would be an artistic break for Joe and a [negative] jolt for Hank," in that Greenberg could expect to see his home run total drop off. "Greenberg, for one, realizes what would happen if he was traded to the Yanks. So he is 'agin it.' He likes Detroit and Briggs Stadium and wants to stay." But the facts seem to refute Greenberg's concerns in this matter since he hit 21 home runs in 96 games at Yankee Stadium. Aside from his home field, that was the third highest amount, ranking behind Sportsman Park in St. Louis where he averaged more than one per game (26 in 100 contests).

The Jewish press, including the *Detroit Jewish Chronicle* and *Chicago Sentinel*, also used the word "agog" in an October story, but with different details: they had the deal as a cash transaction with Gehrig thrown into the mix, ostensibly to also handle the managerial chores. In fact, another source suggested Gehrig would take over as skipper of the Tigers. The next month, *The Sporting News* featured a front-page story that had Gehrig in a straight swap for Greenberg. "True or not, that was an amusing report from New York the other day, regarding a deal between the Tigers and Yankees. It pictured Lou Gehrig going to Col. Jacob Ruppert's bedside to protest against his being traded to Detroit."[24] The article by Sam Greene compared the relative value of the aging Gehrig to Greenberg, who was seven years younger than the Iron Horse. Of course, we know that no such deal was made between the two teams. But it is kind of fun to wonder about "what might have been" had Greenberg been playing in the city with the country's largest Jewish population. Would he have the same degree of success? Would the pressures of playing before his family and friends on a regular basis proved too great a distraction? According to the "Multiverse Theory," somewhere that was (and still is?) a reality.

Monday, September 26, was a rare off day so late in the season. Greenberg had seven games to get the four homers he needed to tie Ruth, or five to wrest the title and be proclaimed the new home run king.

The Tigers were joined by almost 11,000 fans in welcoming the Browns to town for a doubleheader, making up for a previously cancelled contest. In the first game, Greenberg singled in his only official at-bat; he walked the other three times (there go those conspiracy theorists again) in a 5–4 win. But in the nightcap he made the home crowd ecstatic with yet another pair of dingers, both off Billy Cox, a twenty-five-year-old who was technically still a rookie although he was pitching in his third season. That made four times in September and 11 on the year that Greenberg had gone deep twice in the same game, a record that still stands.

Going deep, however, may not be the proper phrase in this instance.

It happened in the very first inning, but there is some discrepancy about just how the ball ended up rolling to the outfield wall. According to John Rosengren's account, "Hank lined the first pitch over second base for what looked like a routine single."[25] But Greenberg, in his memoirs, recalled it as "a long ball over the center fielder's head."[26] Either way, the less-than-speedy slugger ran through Del Baker's stop sign at third base and arrived home at the same time as the ball. Home plate umpire Ed Rommel threw his arms apart indicating "safe." The Browns catcher Sam Harshaney argued stringently, as did manager Ski Melillo, but to no avail. The result: Number 57, in a most un-hammered fashion.

Some forty years later, Greenberg wrote that he received a letter from Harshaney asking him to confirm the story he had been telling his kids: that he had indeed tagged Greenberg out at the plate. Hammerin' Hank could have kept quiet, but he just proved how much of a *mensch* he was.

> I wrote back and said, "I'm sorry. I have no picture [documenting the play], but you are absolutely right. I was out by a mile and had no business being called safe. So you can tell your boys that their dad stopped Hank Greenberg from getting home run number 57."

Although Greenberg inadvertently credited Bill McGowan as the home plate umpire that day rather than Rommel, he could be forgiven. In his memoir he wrote that he made a point of treating all umpires with respect, going out of his way to be civil where most players wouldn't think of breaching that gap.

Greenberg noted that the umpires often stayed at the Leland Hotel, where he and several teammates lived during the season. "So when we were playing at home, I got acquainted with a lot of [them], and we had a different relationship than most ballplayers and umpires have. Once they get to know you and you get to know them, there's no chip on their shoulder when you get out to the ballpark. . . . I think I got my share of calls at home plate."[27] This was one of them. The Elias Bureau may keep track of every pitch and swing nowadays, but that wasn't the case in

Greenberg's time so there's no way to tell how many close calls he actually received because of his kindly attitude toward the men in blue.

The second home run of the nightcap was a more traditional Greenberg wallop, "a lusty clout" as Ward described it, traveling 400 feet into the center-field bleachers to tie Foxx for the second-best single-season total.

Desperate times call for desperate measures. With the Tigers playing out the string, Greenberg didn't have to be as particular or disciplined at the plate. Of course he wanted the Tigers to win, but he also wanted that record. Who wouldn't? That may well have influenced his approach at the plate.

"[B]efore going out on strikes the second time he swung at a bad pitch to avoid being walked on four pitches," Ward wrote in his story about the 12–0 win over the Browns the next day. "He then lifted a drive over the roof of the left field pavilion only to see it go foul a few feet. He missed the next one."

But as had been becoming more of an issue of late, the second game was abbreviated by darkness for the third time in a week. Also noteworthy: September 27 was the second day of Rosh Hashanah, the Jewish New Year.

Four years earlier, Greenberg had become a legend for his decision *not* to do something. Although he would say time and again he was not an observant Jew, he was still compelled by something deeply ingrained to honor the faith of his ancestors. So as the High Holy Days approached, he agonized over what to do: stand by that faith and disappoint his teammates and fans in the midst of as heated pennant race or play and disappoint his family?

After much deliberation, he came to a Solomon-like decision: he would effectively split the difference. The *Detroit News* interviewed Rabbi Joseph Thumin, the religious leader of the city's Temple Beth Abraham, who explained that according to the Talmud—the discussion and interpretation of Jewish law—Rosh Hashanah was a day of celebration, so it was permissible for Greenberg to participate in those games.

This holy dispensation turned out well for all involved: On September 10, 1934, the second day of the holiday, Greenberg hit two home runs in an important 2–1 win over the visiting Boston Red Sox. The first came in the seventh inning to tie the game, the second to lead off the bottom of the ninth for the game winner.

Greenberg would not, however, play on Yom Kippur, which fell on September 19. It turned out to be the only game he missed all year (which also broke a consecutive game streak by the Tigers infield as a whole) and the Tigers lost to the visiting Yankees, 5–2.

Edgar Guest immortalized Greenberg for his courageous stand in "Came Yom Kippur," an ode to the Jewish athlete as told by two Irish fans who figuratively tipped their hats in an uncommon show of inter-religious respect.

The poem, which was published in the October 3 edition of the *Free Press*, concludes:

> Came Yom Kippur—holy fast day world wide over to the Jew,
> And Hank Greenberg to his teaching and the old tradition true
> Spent the day among his people and he didn't come to play.
> Said Murphy to Mulrooney, "We shall lose the game today!

We shall miss him on the infield and shall miss him
at the bat
But he's true to his religion—and I honor him for that!"

Compare Greenberg's mythic holy day experience with the apocryphal story of teammate Harry Eisenstat.

As a rookie pitching for the Brooklyn Dodgers in 1936,
Eisenstat also agonized over whether he should play on the holiday
against their archrivals, the New York Giants (Rosh Hashanah fell
on September 17 that year). Like Greenberg, he sought guidance
from a rabbi who told him it was all right to do his job. Unlike
Greenberg, however, the outcome wasn't as rewarding: Eisenstat
gave up a grand slam to Hank Leiber in the fourth inning of a
17–3 loss in front of his hometown fans at Ebbets Field.

Contrary to the Eisenstat "canon," the home run did not come
on the first pitch he threw. He actually came on in the third
inning with two out in relief of George Jeffcoat, and recorded
the third out without incident. But in the next frame he gave up
a walk, single, and another walk before Leiber struck his blow.
After one more hit, Dodgers skipper Casey Stengel mercifully
pulled him from the game.

Just as the dripping sands of the hourglass in *The Wizard of Oz*
served as a portent for Dorothy's doom, the ensuing games were
incredibly tense, as time was running out on Greenberg's season. The headlines in various papers reflected increasingly grim
updates until the season at last flatlined.

September 28

"Tigers Hit Ball Hard but Hank is Homerless," *Detroit Free Press*; "Greenberg Hitless as Tigers Win, 12–0," *The New York Times*.

September 29

"No Homer for Greenberg," *The New York Times*; "Three Homers in Two Day's is Hank's Job," *Detroit Free Press* (the headline over the game's box score reminded all that *"Tempus Fugit"* when it came to Greenberg's inability to connect).

October 1

"One Day Left for Greenberg," *Detroit Free Press*; "Tribe Stops Tigers and Greenberg," *Cleveland Plain Dealer*; "Greenberg Goes Hitless," *The New York Times*.

October 2

"Hank's Homer Bid Fails," *Detroit Free Press*, "Tribe Stops Tigers and Greenberg," *Cleveland Plain Dealer*.

It was Greenberg's misfortune to have to play out the tail end of the season in Cleveland against the Indians, the only team in the major leagues with two home fields. They hosted the majority of their games at League Park, with its cozy accommodations for just over 21,000 spectators. But for Sundays and holidays, they hiked on over to cavernous Cleveland Municipal Stadium in hopes of taking advantage of its capacity of 72,000. In this case—with the Indians finishing in third place—that didn't happen. A relatively small crowd of 27,000 "came out to watch Hank take pot shots at the home run mark."[28]

Greenberg didn't particularly like playing in Cleveland Stadium. Its dimensions were 320 feet down the left and right field lines—those were fair and definitely reachable—but a daunting 467 feet to the center field wall, exceeded only by two facilities: Philadelphia's Shibe Park, home to both the Phillies and Athletics that year (468 feet), and the New York Giants' fabled Polo Grounds (505 feet).

"It was almost impossible to hit a home run in Municipal Stadium," Greenberg wrote in his memoir. "The distances from home plate were so great that if you didn't drop one down the line, you'd never hit a home run there."[29]

In addition to the architectural impediments, Greenberg "will find the going tough," Ward predicted in his October 1 column as the Tigers prepared for their final series of the '38 season. "For some reason, the Injuns don't seem to be enthusiastic about Hankus. During a game in Detroit, [Indians catcher] Frankie Pytlak was warned by an umpire for allegedly attempting to step on Hank's foot at the plate. It was a timely warning for it would have been too bad for Pytlak if Hank had tried to step on him."[30]

The Indians won the Saturday opener, 5–0, with Greenberg unable to reach base—let alone hit a home run—in four at-bats against Denny Galehouse. Still, with a doubleheader left to hit two home runs, the objective was still in reach. That is, until they saw that Bob Feller was starting the first game.

Greenberg considered "Rapid Robert" one of the toughest pitchers to hit against, but then who didn't? The Hammer came to the plate against his fellow Hall of Famer 79 times—more than all but three pitchers—and struck out 17 times, just one behind Lefty Gomez. He also walked 13 times against Feller, more than any other hurler. Power-wise, Greenberg managed just three home runs off the Indians' star and a .262 batting average. So things were not looking good.

Sure enough, Feller treated the hometown faithful to a dramatic performance on this somewhat overcast day, striking out 18 batters for a new major league record. Unfortunately, he also walked seven and came away with a 4–1 loss. Greenberg struck out twice, received one of Feller's free passes, and scored twice to support Harry Eisenstat's complete-game victory in which he allowed just four hits.

So it all boiled down to this. One game. Still a chance. After all, he'd already hit two homers in one game four times in the month.

But there were a couple of wild cards in the mix. First, it was another nightcap in the team's sixth doubleheader of the month. And while the opener had been completed in a brisk pace of two hours and seven minutes, would they able to complete the finale before the skies darkened?

Second concern: the Indians were starting Johnny Humphries, a pitcher Greenberg had never faced before.

Humphries took the mound in the final game of the season, but his day's work was done before fans had a chance to finish their hot dogs. He allowed five runs on five hits and two walks, including one to Greenberg. His replacement, Clay Smith—in the first of his only two seasons in the majors and another stranger to Greenberg—took over in the second and went the rest of the way. Hank enjoyed Smith's company, smacking three hits—all singles—and drawing another walk in the 10–8 Tigers win in seven innings. It was the only time they would face each other. After returning to the minors for two more years, Smith made his second and final big league stint as Greenberg's teammate in 1940.

It was somewhat ironic: had the Tigers not put up much offense in the first and had they not allowed the Indians to claw back, perhaps they could have gotten in the remaining innings. But, sadly for Greenberg, his teammates, the city of Detroit, and fans in general, the umpires had no choice but to shut it down.

The *Cleveland Plain Dealer* prominently featured Feller's performance on their front page the next day along with a photo. But Hank's hometown paper did not see fit to offer similar treatment to the Tigers' victories or Greenberg's accomplishments on theirs. In fact, the *Free Press* story began somewhat uncharitably, considering the thrills he had provided in an otherwise drab campaign: "Hank Greenberg's attempt to break Babe Ruth's major league home-run record ended in brilliant failure today . . ."[31]

John Rosengren speculated in his Greenberg biography that the shortened games at the end of the season "cost Greenberg valuable at-bats. All told, Hank probably lost 20 at-bats to rain or darkness that season, which translated into at least two homers, given his season average of a home run every 9.6 at-bats."[32]

According to Matt Rothenberg, manager of the Giamatti Research Center at the National Baseball Hall of Fame Library in Cooperstown, New York, whether Greenberg was disadvantaged by those shortened nightcaps is a question of at least some debate.

Based on the box scores on Baseball-Reference.com and failing to find play-by-plays for these games through the Library's

ProQuest newspapers data, Rothenberg attempted to suss out additional chances for plate appearances in those shortened contests late in the last three weeks of the season. He shared his findings in an email which serves as the basis for the following scenarios.

September 21, a 3–0 win over the A's, called after five innings: Baseball-Reference.com says the A's pitcher Buck Ross faced 24 batters in five innings. Going through the Detroit lineup, that means the last batter he faced was Fox. That means, provided the Tigers went down in order, it would have at least been:

Sixth inning: Billy Rogell, Mark Christman, and the pitcher's spot
Seventh inning: Chet Morgan, Dixie Walker, Charlie Gehringer
Eighth inning: Greenberg, Rudy York, Pete Fox
Ninth inning: Rogell, Christman, and the pitcher's spot

Naturally, there are many assumptions which must first be made, but Greenberg seems assured of at least one more plate appearance had the game gone nine innings (or eight-and-a-half).

September 23, a 6–5 loss to the Indians, called after seven innings: Baseball-Reference.com says the Indians starter Earl Whitehill faced 25 batters in 5.1 innings and reliever Johnny Humphries faced eight in 1.2 innings. Provided the Tigers go down in order, it would have at least been:

Eighth inning: Rogell, Christman, and the pitcher's spot
Ninth inning: Roy Cullenbine, Chet Laabs, Gehringer

In this case, there is no guarantee Greenberg gets that one additional plate appearance. It is certainly possible that it could happen, however.

September 27, a 10–2 win over the Browns, called after seven innings: Baseball-Reference.com says the Browns starter Billy Cox faced 24 batters in five innings and reliever Ed Cole faced nine batters in two innings. Provided the Tigers go down in order, it would have been:

Eighth inning: Birdie Tebbetts, Christman, and the pitcher's spot
Ninth inning: Morgan, Walker, Gehringer

Again, in this case, there is no guarantee Greenberg gets that one additional plate appearance. Plus, if the Tigers go down in order in the eighth, they would have to blow a big lead to a lousy team at home to come up in the ninth.

October 2, a 10–8 win over the Indians, called after seven innings: Starter Humphries faced nine batters in one inning and reliever Cole Smith faced 25 batters in six innings. Provided the Tigers go down in order, it would have been:

Eighth inning: Christman, the pitcher's spot, and Benny McCoy
Ninth inning: Fox, Cullenbine, Greenberg

In this case, it is likely Greenberg would have at least one more plate appearance. The Tigers were on the road, so they would have batted in the ninth.

Again, each scenario is based on several assumptions of certain occurrences happening or not happening. Provided the batters-faced statistic is accurate in all four games, Greenberg seems assured of having at least two more plate appearances.[33]

Years later, Greenberg reminisced about the end of the season and just falling short of one of the most revered of records.

"Some people still have it fixed in their minds that the reason I didn't break Ruth's record was, because I was Jewish, the ballplayers did everything they could to stop me," Greenberg told Lawrence Ritter for *The Glory of Their Times*, the classic collection of oral history by ballplayers in the first half of the twentieth century. "That's pure baloney. The fact of the matter is quite the opposite: so far as I could tell, the players were mostly rooting for me, aside from the pitchers. . . . The reason I didn't hit 60 or 61 is that I ran out of gas."[34]

"I once asked Hank about [the conspiracy]," wrote Ira Berkow in a column following Greenberg's death in 1986. "'Not true,' he said. 'I got some hits and hit some balls, but I couldn't get them over the fence,' he said. 'In fact, there were people in baseball rooting for me to break the record.' He recalled trying for an inside-the-park homer late in the season in which the umpire called him safe at home, 'when I was really out.'"[35]

Greenberg's contentions have been contested by writers and analysts who believe he was just being polite. He was too classy to use anti-Semitism as an alibi, they said, just as he had counseled

Harry Eisenstat. Over the years he repeated his position that he didn't want to be known as a Jewish athlete, but an athlete who happened to be Jewish. He seemed to reverse course when he was interviewed by Ritter.

> I realize now, more than I used to, how important a part I played in the lives of a generation of Jewish kids who grew up in the thirties. I never thought about it then. But in recent years, men I meet often tell me how much I meant to them when they were growing up. It's almost the first thing a lot of them say to me. It still surprises me to hear it, but I think I'm finally starting to believe it.[36]

In an article in *The New York Times'* "Keeping Score" column, Howard Megdal, author of *The Baseball Talmud: The Definitive Position-by-Position Ranking of Baseball's Chosen People*, among other baseball books, contradicted Greenberg's beliefs. He claimed that anti-Semitism *was* most likely responsible for the failure at a fair shot at the record. "Evidence has finally been published that seems to resolve a seventy-two-year-old mystery. When Hank Greenberg of the Detroit Tigers made a run at Babe Ruth's season home run record, falling two short with 58 in 1938, was he pitched around because he was Jewish?"

"The American League didn't seem exactly thrilled with Greenberg's pursuit," Megdal wrote.[37]

The "evidence" came in the form of game logs published by Retrosheet.org (now available via BaseballReference.com). "Until the Web site Retrosheet.org recently published game logs for the

1938 season, the subject of anti-Semitism during Greenberg's record chase was a matter of opinion."

By poring over the logs, Megdal determined that using only the cold objetive numbers, Greenberg received more than the normal amount of walks, indicating the opposition's reluctance to give him a shot over the final weeks of the season.

"[T]he statistical record stands as evidence that Greenberg's religion might have been an additional barrier," Megdal concluded.

But by using the word "might," does Megdal somehow lessen the impact of his assertion? Several other analysts have disagreed with his findings, sometimes taking great (and discourteous) pains to show him wrong. Some refuted his charges of anti-Semitism, others his methodology. As Megdal alluded in the article, one can never truly know what is in the heart, mind, and/or soul of another man (discounting out-and-out lunatics like Hitler and his ilk), so it's difficult to be able to say with 100 percent certainty one way or the other. And I admit my own limited analytical skills in the appendix is less of a definitive answer than a possible consideration. But perhaps it might serve to shed some light that, on the surface, there was nothing extraordinary about the way opponents pitched to Greenberg in the last few weeks of 1938.

In the end, the reasons and analysis don't matter. Hammerin' Hank came up short. It was an exhausting experience, but at the end of the day it's all relative, isn't it? Compared to what Greenberg and the rest of the world would soon have to deal with, hitting a ball with a stick didn't seem all that important.

Greenberg's season was over, but he still popped up in the news for playing baseball that year, taking part in a doubleheader back in his native New York just one week later. He hit two doubles for the Bushwicks in their 2–1 win over the Bay Parkways and was held without a hit in the darkness-shortened nightcap (no score reported). He wasn't the only one with major league experience playing: Ex-Yankee Waite Hoyt and Izzy Goldstein, Greenberg's fellow alumnus from James Monroe High School and a member of the 1932 Tigers—his only season in the Bigs— combined for the win.

Greenberg in September–October:

G	PA	AB	R	H	2B	3B	HR	RBI	BB	SO	BA	OBP	SLG
32	137	109	35	38	5	0	12	34	28	20	.349	.482	.725

Greenberg in 1938 (through October 2):

G	PA	AB	R	H	2B	3B	HR	RBI	BB	SO	BA	OBP	SLG
155	681	556	144	175	23	4	58	147	119	92	.315	.438	.683

Notes

1 *Story of My Life*, p. 120.
2 Marty Appel, *Pinstripe Empire: The New York Yankees from Before the Babe to After the Boss* (Bloomsbury, 2012), p. 339.
3 John Lardner, "Greenberg Gunning to Outdo Babe." *Hartford Courant*, September 2, 1938.
4 Abraham Cahan, "Should Children Play Baseball." *Daily Jewish Forward*, August 6, 1903.

5   "Hankus-Pankus." *Boston Jewish Advocate*, September 2, 1938.

6   Charles P. Ward, "Ward to the Wise." *Detroit Free Press*, September 2, 1938.

7   *Story of My Life*, p. 117.

8   Ibid, p. 120.

9   Charles P. Ward, "Hank Blasts Out No. 50 as Tigers Sweep Series." *Detroit Free Press*, September 13, 1938.

10 Richards Vidmer, "Down in Front." *New York Herald Tribune*, September 14, 1938.

11 *Detroit Free Press*, September 16, 1938.

12 Richards Vidmer, "Down in Front." *Washington Post*, September 16, 1938.

13 *Story of My Life*, p. 101.

14 *Hero of Heroes*, p. 169.

15 *Detroit Free Press*, September 17, 1938.

16 Bill James, *The New Bill James Historical Baseball Abstract* (Free Press, 2001), p. 891.

17 James P. Dawson, "Greenberg Drives Nos. 52 and 53 As Tigers Score, 7–3, Over Yankees." *The New York Times*, September 18, 1938.

18 *Detroit Free Press*, September 18, 1938.

19 Charles P. Ward, "Hank Five Homers from mark with 9 Games to Go." *Detroit Free Press*, September 24, 1938.

20 Charles P. Ward, "Ward to the Wise." *Detroit Free Press*, September 25, 1938.

21 James E. Doyle, "H'only One Babe." "The Sports Trail," *Cleveland Plain Dealer*, September 24, 1938.

22 *Detroit Free Press*, September, 26, 1938.

23 *Detroit Free Press*, September 25, 1938.

24 Sam Greene, "Iron Horse Story Fiction to Detroit." *The Sporting News*, November 17, 1938.

25 *Hero of Heroes*, p. 172.

26 *Story of My Life*, p. 113.

27 Ibid, p. 106.

28 "Hank's Homer Bid Fails—Feller Fans 18 for Record." *Detroit Free Press*, October 3, 1938.

29 *Story of My Life*, p. 99.

30 Charles P. Ward, "Ward to the Wise." *Detroit Free Press*, October 1, 2918.

31 *Detroit Free Press*, October 3, 1938.

32 *Hero of Heroes*, p. 169.

33 Email from Matt Rothenberg, August 22, 2016.

34 Lawrence Ritter, *The Glory of Their Times* (Harper Perennial, 1992), p. 317.

35 Ira Berkow, "Greenberg: Kind of a Beacon." *The New York Times*, September 7, 1986.

36 *The Glory of Their Times*, p. 330.

37 "Religion Aided a Home Run Chase, and May Have Led to Its Failure." *The New York Times*, March 20, 2010.

BEYOND '38

"Maybe Jimmie Foxx will break that record of sixty home runs. Maybe Joe DiMaggio or Rudy York or Hal Trosky or Bill Dickey will break it. Maybe I will. That won't make any of us a second Babe Ruth."
—Hank Greenberg in *Collier's* magazine[1]

Richards Vidmer, that old killjoy, was right.

Despite his overall success and the thrills he gave to baseball fans (as well as non-fans), Greenberg finished third behind Red Sox slugger Jimmie Foxx and Bill Dickey, the stalwart Yankees catcher, in the American League MVP voting. It wasn't all that surprising, despite the excitement of the home run chase. Greenberg topped both leagues in that department. He also led in runs (143) and tied for bases on balls with Foxx and Dolph Camilli of the Brooklyn Dodgers. To be fair, Foxx's credentials were most impressive. His 50 homers were second in baseball and he led the majors in total bases (398) and on-base and slugging percentages (.462 and .704, respectively) while winning the junior circuit batting title with a .349 average. Dickey, on the other hand, didn't come out on top in a single category, but as the backbone of the pennant-winning Yankees earned a great deal of respect from the writers. Foxx picked up 19 first place votes while Dickey earned the other three.

Years layer, Greenberg reflected in his memoirs, "When you're playing, awards don't seem like much. Then you get older and all of it becomes more precious. It is nice to be remembered."

It stood to reason to think that Greenberg would not be able to repeat his 1938 success. After all, until 1961 no one hit more home runs than he had. Only four players even reached 50 in that interim: Mickey Mantle (52 in 1956), Ralph Kiner (54 in 1949 and 51 in 1947), Johnny Mize (51 in 1947), and Willie Mays (51 in 1955).

Greenberg appeared in 138 games in 1939, hitting 33 home runs and driving in a disappointing—for him, at least—113 runs. More distressing to his pride was that he topped the league in strikeouts with 95, a figure more than a few modern-day sluggers might rack up by the All-Star break. Greenberg considering going down on strikes a source of embarrassment. Babe Ruth had no such qualms in that regard. He loved to brag about his long shots and his approach at the plate. "I swing as hard as I can, and I try to swing right through the ball. The harder you grip the bat, the more you can swing it through the ball, and the farther the ball will go. I swing big, with everything I've got. I hit big or I miss big. I like to live as big as I can." His philosophy was simple: "Never let the fear of striking out get in your way."[2]

Greenberg, on the other hand, looked at it as a shortcoming, an evidence of poor judgment and self-control. "A bad day for

Charlie [Gehringer] would be one strikeout—one strikeout! I'd be flailing away at the ball, looking very foolish at the plate. . ."[3]

Greenberg was not alone in his downswing; the entire league fell off from the previous year:

Average Per Team

Year	Runs/RPG	HR	RBI	Slash
1938	823/5.37	108	776	.281/.358/.415
1939	801/5.21	100	745	.279/.352/.407

Nevertheless, Greenberg's 33 home runs were good enough for second place in the major leagues, just two behind Foxx. The Tigers fell to a fifth-place finish with a record of 81–73. Bobo Newsom and Tommy Bridges each won 17 games, but no other starter finished above .500.

Greenberg won the home run crown again in 1940 and led the AL in RBIs with a tidy 150 to go along with 50 doubles, a .670 slugging percentage, and an OPS (on-base plus slugging percentage) of 1.103, all of which led the junior circuit and netted him his second MVP award. The Tigers won the pennant by a single game over the Indians and he enjoyed the kind of World Series he had missed in 1935, leading the team with 10 hits—including two doubles, a triple, and one of their four home runs—for a .357 batting average. He also had six RBIs to tie Pinky Higgins for tops among Tigers. But his individual success didn't translate to a world championship, as Detroit lost to the Cincinnati Reds in seven games.

Charles Lindbergh was still a hero to the people of the United States. Not only did the handsome flyer complete the first solo transatlantic flight in 1927—the year of that other famous record—he also became a sympathetic figure following the kidnapping and murder of his infant son five years later.

The case became a national sensation. In 1934, Bruno Richard Hauptmann, an itinerant carpenter, was arrested and charged with the "crime of the century." He was tried, sentenced, and executed two years later. The painful memories clung to the Lindbergh family so much so that they moved to Europe to escape the spotlight.

It was during this period that Lindbergh, an international celebrity for his daring feat, was invited by France and Germany to inspect their air forces for his valued opinion. He thought France was a disorganized mess but declared his favorable impression of the Nazi war machine. As a token of their admiration, Germany presented him with one of their highest honors, the Service Cross of the Order of the Eagle with Star— somewhat fitting since one of Lindbergh's nicknames was the Lone Eagle.

The award did not sit well with many Americans, who regarded Lindbergh as a misguided stooge of the Nazi regime, especially as he became a more vocal advocate of the America First movement, determined to keep the United States out of any foreign wars. In addition, the fact that he aligned himself with Henry Ford did not comfort the Jewish population, whom Lindbergh—like Ford—blamed for many of the country's ills.

Like Lindbergh, Hitler considered Ford a fellow traveler, someone who shared the same ideas—albeit perhaps with a less violent endgame—about inferior races. Ford, too, was the recipient of the

Service Cross, bestowed upon him by the German consuls from Detroit and Cleveland in honor of his seventy-fifth birthday on July 30, 1938. It was the first time the honor had been made inside the United States. Ironically, that was the same day Greenberg and Eisenstat—members of one of those "inferior races"—joined forces to sweep a double header against the Philadelphia A's.

Ford came under a lot of pressure to renounce the prize. Eddie Cantor, one of the most popular entertainers in the US at the time, asked, "Whose side is Mr. Ford on? . . . I don't think he is a real American or a good Christian. The more men like Ford we have the more we must organize and fight."

Cantor had recently returned from England where he participated in a drive to raise $500,000 to help send refugee children to Palestine, as Israel was known before it became an independent country in 1948. He offered an ominous warning to his fellow Jewish-Americans: "We can smell the smoke in this country and we've go to start now to save ourselves. Don't think we're safe here, because we are not. And we can't fight Hitler just fifteen minutes a day when he is working twenty-four hours."[4]

A few days later, the Jewish War Veterans released a statement directed at Ford decrying the award as an "act on your part [that] can only be interpreted as an endorsement by you of the barbarous, indecent and irreligious Nazi program and philosophy." The organization implored him "in the name of humanity and Americanism" to "repudiate that award and all it stands for."[5]

For his part, Ford tried to nullify the bad press, knowing it could negatively affect his auto business, which was already hurting. After a meeting with Rabbi Leo Franklin, a highly respected spiritual leader in Detroit, Ford issued a press release stating his

belief that the US should open its doors to refugees and denying
his sympathy for Hitler and the Nazis.

> My acceptance of a medal from the German people does
> not, as some people seem to think, involve any sympathy
> on my part with nazism [sic]. Those who have known me
> for many years realize that anything that breeds hate is
> repulsive to me.
>
> I am confident that the time is near when there will be
> so many jobs available in this country that the entrance
> of a few thousand Jews, or others, will be negligible.

At the same time, he couldn't help a few backhanded compli-
ments regarding Jews.

> Because of their special adaptability in the fields of pro-
> duction, distribution and agriculture they would offer
> to the business of this country a new impetus at a time
> like this, when it is badly needed. Hundreds of Jewish
> men now employed in our plants show marked ability
> and loyalty, and if the turnover among them is sometimes
> comparatively high, it is indicative of their ambition to
> improve themselves.[6]

Greenberg had been following the news reports enough to believe
it was only a matter of time before the United States was forced
to enter the fray. As the 1941 season opened, he decided to enter
the military of his own accord rather than wait to be drafted.

The press proclaimed him an unselfish hero for giving up a new contract that would have paid him $50,000 for the $50-a-month salary a soldier received. Greenberg said all the right things: that he was proud to serve, that he understood that as a thirty-year-old this could have a deleterious effect on his career. Nevertheless, the situation warranted the sacrifice.

Greenberg appeared in just 19 games for the Tigers before leaving for basic training. He hit only two home runs but they were among the most dramatic of his career, rivaling the pair he had hit on the Jewish New Year in 1934 to beat the Red Sox during that year's pennant chase.

Both came in a single game, the May 6 contest with the Yankees at Briggs Stadium—his last before reporting for duty the following day. Perhaps the last of his career. The first was a solo shot into the left field stands to open the second inning and give the Tigers a 1–0 lead. Home run number two went to the same spot in the fourth with York on base to extend the lead to 4–0, en route to a 7–4 win. Unfortunately, fewer than 8,000 spectators were on hand to bid him farewell and Godspeed. The *Free Press* ran a series of photos of Greenberg on the back page saying goodbye: to the fans, to his teammates, to his manager Del Baker, and to Tigers' owner Walter Briggs.

Greenberg's draft board had actually given him permission to delay reporting so he could attend the flag-raising cere-mony to honor the 1940 World Championship team prior to the next day's game against the Washington Senators but Greenberg declined, content to go out on that high note and get his army career going. "I was ordered to report for military service at 6:30 o'clock [sic] Wednesday morning. I'll be there," he said.[7] "If there is any last message to be given the public, let it be that I'm going to be a good soldier," Greenberg told *The Sporting News*.[8]

He could have played it safe. Plenty of athletes had entered the various branches of the service and received cushy jobs as morale officers or fitness instructors, a dodge that would allow them to continue to play ball for military teams. Despite some grumbling from non-sports fans about preferential treatment, these athletes often served as boosters, giving their fellow servicemen a taste of home during perilous times. Greenberg, however, insisted on active duty. He was assigned to C Company, 2nd Infantry, 5th Division in Fort Custer, Louisiana, where he received training as an anti-tank gunner, rising to the rank of sergeant.

Racism and anti-Semitism were as much a part of the military as they were in baseball or any other institution. It was not until 1948, when President Harry S. Truman issued Executive Order 9981, that African American and Caucasian troops were allowed to serve in the same units. Greenberg had to deal with the same backward thinking he encountered in the minor leagues, mostly from boys from the South who had never met a Jew. One apocryphal story has a drunken loudmouth asking if there were any Ginsburgs or Goldbergs around for him to beat up. The former Tiger stood up to his full six-foot-three height and said, "My name is Greenberg. Will I do?" The soldier quickly sobered up and said he wasn't looking for a Greenberg, just a Goldberg or Ginsburg.

In August, Congress ordered the release from service of men aged twenty-eight and older. Greenberg received his discharge on December 5, after just a little over six months of duty. He was on his way back to New York when the Japanese bombed Pearl Harbor. With a minimum of thought, Greenberg made the decision to re-enter the armed forces.

As for the rest of the sport, Commissioner Landis sent a letter to FDR in January 1942. "The time is approaching when, in ordinary conditions, our teams would be heading for spring training camps," he wrote to the president. "However, inasmuch as these are not ordinary times, I venture to ask what you have in mind as to whether professional baseball should continue to operate."

Roosevelt's quick response, which came to be known as the "Green Light Letter," remains an indication of the importance of the national pastime to the American identity.

> As you will, of course, realize the final decision about the baseball season must rest with you and the Baseball club owners—so what I am going to say is solely a personal and not an official point of view.
>
> I honestly feel that it would be best for the country to keep baseball going. There will be fewer people unemployed and everybody will work longer hours and harder than ever before.
>
> And that means that they ought to have a chance for recreation and for taking their minds off their work even more than before.
>
> Baseball provides a recreation which does not last over two hours or two hours and a half, and which can be got for very little cost. And, incidentally, I hope that night games can be extended because it gives an opportunity to the day shift to see a game occasionally.

As to the players themselves, I know you agree with me that the individual players who are active military or naval age should go, without question, into the services. Even if the actual quality to the teams is lowered by the greater use of older players, this will not dampen the popularity of the sport. Of course, if an individual has some particular aptitude in a trade or profession, he ought to serve the Government. That, however, is a matter which I know you can handle with complete justice.

Here is another way of looking at it—if 300 teams use 5,000 or 6,000 players, these players are a definite recreational asset to at least 20,000,000 of the fellow citizens—and that in my judgment is thoroughly worthwhile.

Dissatisfied with his experience in the infantry, Greenberg enlisted in the Army Air Force. Initially, he was utilized as a physical instructor and did play a little ball, but he was soon transferred to Officers Candidate School where he earned the rank of captain. In 1944, he requested an overseas posting and was assigned to serve in the China-Burma-India Theater of Operations. He served in the CBI for a few months before being recalled to the United States where he served as a liaison officer, giving returned veterans tours of war production plants.

Upon his honorable discharge, Greenberg decided to see if he could still make an impact on the baseball diamond.

Greenberg's return to baseball on July 1, 1945, was just as "Hollywood" as his last game before entering the service. "Thrills were what 48,811 fans sought at Briggs Stadium. They got 'em," was the way Lyall Smith opened his story in the *Detroit Free Press* the next day.[9] Greenberg started the opener of the double-header against the visiting Philadelphia A's, returning to both left field and his old cleanup spot in the batting order. After being retired in his first three at-bats and working out a walk, he sure did give the Briggs Stadium faithful a thrill they would tell their kids about when he socked a home run off reliever Charlie Gassaway in a 9–5 Tigers victory. The *Free Press* featured his picture on page one with the subhead of the story announcing "Greenberg Back in the Old Groove."

The team, now under the direction of manager Steve O'Neill, was already in first place with a record of 38–24, 3.5 games over the Yankees. Not that it was an easy going. No, sir. The Tigers found themselves in a down-to-the-wire battle—not with the New Yorkers, but the Washington Senators. The two teams fought it out until the very end, which came courtesy, once again, of Captain Greenberg.

On September 30—the last day of the season—the Tigers found themselves on the down side end of 3–2 score against the Browns at Sportsman's Park heading into the top of the ninth. Hub Walker, pinch-hitting for pitcher Hal Newhouser, led off with a single. Skeeter Webb sought to move him along with a sacrifice but both men were safe as Walker beat the throw to second. After Walker was replaced by pinch runner Red Borom, Eddie Mayo succeeded in his bunt attempt, putting runners on second and third. The Browns elected to walk Doc Cramer intentionally, bringing Greenberg to the plate.

The count was one ball and one strike on Hank, the man who came back from four years in the service of his country to play baseball.

[Nels] Potter wound up and threw a high fast one toward the plate. Hank hit the ball on a line out of the field into the left stands at the 351-foot mark to drive home Red Borom, Skeeter Webb and Doc Cramer.

By the time Hank reached home plate, he was caught up in a maelstrom of humanity that was every Tiger on the team. He was hugged and roughed and kissed and pummeled.[10]

"Hank's Bat Wins Flag," screamed the October 1 *Free Press* headline. So much for those concerns about losing his skills.

Greenberg appeared in 78 games after his discharge. He contributed 13 home runs and 60 RBIs with a slash line of .311/.404/.544, which earned him 14th place in the AL MVP voting, an outstanding accomplishment for such an abbreviated season.

It was almost anti-climactic, but the Tigers beat the Cubs in the World Series, four games to three. Greenberg batted .304 with two homers and seven RBIs. Chicago had been happy with the AL outcome because it meant a bigger share of the World Series pot, even if they were to lose. "A packed house at Detroit is expected to give the Cubs slice one-third more money than they would have received had Washington won," according to an AP story once the Tigers secured the pennant.[11]

Baseball pundits love to speculate, to ask "what if?"

What if Lou Gehrig hadn't contracted the disease that would one day bear his name, forcing him out of the game when he still might have had some good years left?

What if Pete Reiser, the Brooklyn Dodgers wunderkind, hadn't been such a hard-nosed player, running into outfield walls with such abandon it nearly cost him his life on one occasion?

On the flip side, what if contemporary players, more or less assured of Hall of Fame consideration, hadn't allegedly used performance enhancing drugs, making a mockery of the records books with inflated statistics?

And what if men like Hank Greenberg, Bob Feller, and Ted Williams didn't have to give up prime playing years because men like Adolf Hitler, Benito Mussolini, and Emperor Hirohito dragged the world into a devastating calamity?

In his 2005 article "War Begone," published on the *Hardball Times* website, Steve Treder tried to answer that last question. He examined a number of batters and, using advanced sabermetrics, concluded that Greenberg might have had an additional 171 home runs and 543 RBIs in the three full and two partial seasons he missed. All things being equal—that is, assuming Greenberg didn't suffer from any injuries or other issues that prevented him from reaching Treder's final figures—this is what his stats might have looked like when he retired.

	HR	RBI
Actual	331	1,274
Projected	502	1,817

And that doesn't even take into consideration the missed income that such lofty accomplishments would have garnered the players.[17]

But these members of the Greatest Generation, who had all the right in the world to gripe about the interruption in what is by necessity a short-lived career, did not complain. To do so would have been unseemly, with the press ready to pounce on such un-American behavior. When Mickey Mantle was determined unfit to serve in the Korean War because of the osteomyelitis he had suffered as a football player in school, he was pilloried by the media. How could this strapping young man be healthy enough to play for the Yankees but not be part of the "Yanks" fighting forces, they asked?

Baseball, after all, is just a game.

Actually, it's not. Baseball, like all sports, is a business of "what have you done for me lately." After Greenberg's inspirational return helped Detroit win a world's championship, he played one more full season there, leading the AL in home runs with 44 and RBIs with 127 as the Tigers finished in second place, 12 games behind the Red Sox.

Despite these numbers, the front office considered Greenberg an "old" thirty-five and no longer what they needed or wanted— certainly not at his $55,000 base salary (plus another $20,000 in deferred payments, according to John Rosengren's account), which was among the highest in the game.

After all his sacrifice, after all the thrills he had given the fans both on the field and as the epitome of a solid citizen, as a symbol to the Jewish community and a hero for all, the Tigers gave Greenberg the ultimate insult (or compliment, depending on your point of view): they waived him out of the league. The Yankees had expressed interest, believing he could pull in Jewish fans, but Briggs and company were not about to let that happen. They would not put themselves in a position where Greenberg could come back and haunt them on a well-timed home run or similarly dramatic event.

The Pittsburgh Pirates picked him up for $10,000. He learned the news via telegram.

> This is to inform you that your contract has been purchased by the Pitsburgh club of the National League Trust you will find your new connection a most profitable one [sic].[13]

In his memoirs, Greenberg expressed his shock, not just *by* the news, but with the way it was delivered. "After having spent sixteen years in the Detroit organization," he wrote, "to get that kind of telegram left me speechless."[14]

He considered retiring. Like many military veterans returning to civilian life, Greenberg realized there were more important things; baseball had become almost trivial. He'd made a good living as an athlete. He was smart. He would land on his feet, aided by the love of his wife, Caral Gimbel, heiress to the famous department store chain who he'd married in 1945.

Greenberg initially told the Pirates he didn't want to play. He was concerned that he wouldn't be able to match his traditional home run prowess at Forbes Field, where the left field wall was 360 feet away. But they sought him not only for his athletic skills, which were admittedly on the wane, but also for his leadership, especially when it came to mentoring their young slugger

Ralph Kiner. He relented after they agreed to several concessions including a $100,000 contract, making him the highest-paid player in the game, as well as a private suite on the road. Perhaps most impressive, the Pirates reconfigured their ball park, moving in the fences to 340 feet to match the distance at Briggs Stadium.

Whatever he did by way of tutoring the next generation or by example, it worked. In his final big-league season where he had to face an entirely new set of pitchers, Greenberg hit 25 home runs and drove in 74 runs in 125 games. Kiner, then in his second big league season, led the National League in home runs for seven straight years. He had accumulated 369 homers when he retired at the age of thirty-two due to a bad back and was inducted into the Hall of Fame in 1975.

Kiner often praised Greenberg for his kindness, patience, and wisdom. The two became fast friends. In his 2004 memoir, *Baseball Forever: Reflections on 60 Years in the Game*, Kiner credited Greenberg as "the biggest single influence in my adult life." They were so close that Greenberg served as Kiner's best man—*twice.* The third time Kiner got married, Greenberg declined the honor, saying he didn't want to jinx the nuptials.[15]

Notes

1 Hank Greenberg, "How to Hit a Home Run." *Collier's* magazine, April 22, 1939.

2 Babe Ruth Quotes (baberuth.com/quotes).

3 *An Illustrated History*, p. 76.

4 "Nazi Honor to Ford Stirs Cantor's Ire." *The New York Times*, August 4, 1938.

5 "Urge Ford to Reject German Decoration." *The New York Times*, August 7, 1938.

6   "Ford for U.S. as Refugee Haven; Denies Sympathy With Nazism." *The New York Times*, December 1, 1938.

7   Charles P. Ward, "Greenberg Bids Farewell with 2 Homers as Yankees Fall, 7 to 4." *Detroit Free Press*, May 7, 1941.

8   "Scribbled by Scribes." *The Sporting News*, May 15, 1941.

9   "Rudy, Hank Homer as Tigers Trounce A's, 9–5, 4–3." *Detroit Free Press*, July 2, 1945.

10   *Detroit Free Press*, October 1, 1945.

11   "Cubs Have Hero, Too – It's Greenberg." *Detroit Free Press*, October 1, 1945.

12   Ted Williams' numbers are even more impressive, given that he lost four seasons to World War II between the ages of 23 and 26) plus *another* two during the Korean War (ages 33–34). Treder calculated the Splendid Splinter would have finished his career as the greatest player who ever lived at that time, something Williams had frequently said was his aspiration, with 709 home runs, second only to the Babe until Hank Aaron came along; 2,429 runs batted in; and a slash line of .346/.485/.645, all at or near the best in the history of the game to that point.

13   *Story of My Life*, p. 176.

14   Ibid, p. 197.

15   Official Website of Hank Greenberg, "Extra Endnotes." (hankgreenberg.net/extra-endnotes)

THE FINAL (CLASS) ACT

"Class tells. It sticks out all over Mr. Greenberg."
—Jackie Robinson[1]

As John Rosengren points out in his biography, Hank Greenberg had to be one of the loneliest men in the game.

". . . [W]hile the Italians and Irish had other teammates to help them absorb the epithets of 'wops' and 'mics,' Greenberg was usually the only Jew on the field to weather the cries of 'kike!' 'I was singled out all the time,' he said. 'Being Jewish and the object of a lot of derogatory remarks keep me on my toes all the time. I could never relax and be one of the boys.'"[2]

If Greenberg felt that way, imagine what Jackie Robinson had to go through.

Greenberg's final season, 1947, was Robinson's first. In his memoirs, the Jewish ballplayer expressed a good deal of empathy for the Brooklyn Dodger rookie, the first African American to break the color barrier. "I couldn't help but admire him," he wrote.

When the Dodgers paid their first visit of the season to Pittsburgh in mid-May. Greenberg was chagrined at the appalling treatment his teammates extended Robinson.

> "I got to thinking, here were our guys, a bunch of ignorant, stupid Southerners who couldn't speak properly, who hadn't graduated from school, and all they could do was make jokes about Jackie. They couldn't recognize that they had a special person in front of them, a gem. They just kept ragging him and calling him names."[3]

Details surrounding their fateful encounter vary, but here are the basics. In the May 15 series opener, Robinson laid down a bunt and inadvertently crashed into Greenberg— back at his old position of first base—when the pitcher's throw went awry. Fans held their collective breath to see if there would be any sort of confrontation between the two men. If they were hoping for a violent display, they were disappointed.

Specifics about the timing of Greenberg's expression of support and empathy are somewhat sketchy. Perhaps it came right after the moment of impact or maybe it was later, when Greenberg wound up on first base as the result of a walk (although Robinson spent the majority of his career as a second baseman, he was initially played at first in his inaugural campaign). The Pirate newcomer struck up the dialogue, asking Robinson if he was all right from their run-in and telling him, in effect, to "hang in there."

I said to Robinson . . . "don't pay attention to these Southern jockeys. They aren't worth anything as far as you're concerned."

He thanked me and I said, "Would you like to go to dinner?"

He said, "I'd love to go to dinner, but I shouldn't because it would put you on the spot."

That was our conversation, and we were always friends after that.[4]

A day or so later, the Associated Press reported a slightly different version of the episode.

Jackie Robinson . . . has picked a diamond hero—rival First Baseman Hank Greenberg of the Pittsburgh Pirates.

Here's why:

Robinson and Greenberg collided in a play at first base during the current Dodgers-Pirates series. The next time up Jackie came down to the sack and Hank said:

"I forgot to ask you if you were hurt in that play."

Assured that Robinson was unharmed, Greenberg said: "Stick in there. You're doing fine. Keep your chin up."

This encouragement from an established star heartened Robinson who has been the subject of reported anti-racial treatment elsewhere and admits he has undergone "jockeying—some of it pretty severe."

"Class tells. It sticks out all over Mr. Greenberg," Robinson declared.[5]

Although the incident did not achieve the same legendary status of Pee Wee Reese, the Kentucky-born Dodgers shortstop, draping his arm around Robinson in a show of support in front of hostile fans in Cincinnati, Greenberg's kind gesture and Robinson's grateful response was in itself a symbol of the symbiotic relationship between two communities that were the subject of frequent scorn and prejudice. (Robert Cottrell covers their similar situations in his excellent dual-biography, *Two Pioneers: How Hank Greenberg and Jackie Robinson Transformed Baseball—and America.*)

Greenberg's baseball career didn't end when he retired at the conclusion of the season. The following year, he bought a piece of the Indians and became the team's general manager under his friend Bill Veeck. Cleveland won the AL pennant that year and again in 1954, posting one of the best records in the history, 111–43.

As the Indians GM, Greenberg was shocked at treatment afforded to the black members of the team. In his memoirs, he recalled making a road trip with the team to Baltimore.

> I waited until all the players had left the bus and then I found myself standing there with five players. They were not going to the hotel because they were black. It hadn't occurred to me that these players would not be admitted to the hotel. . . . I thought to myself, This is terrible. Here these fellows are a vital part of the team and contributing greatly to the success of the team, and they have to be segregated and are not permitted into the hotel to spend the night.

He also learned that the same deal applied in Washington, DC. Greenberg instructed the traveling secretary, who set up the accommodations when the team was on the road, that henceforth such arrangements would not be tolerated. "This is not going on any longer. In 1956 we are going to write to every hotel before the season opens and tell them that we will not send our team there unless everyone on the team is accepted and treated as a guest with the same equal rights."

Sportswriter Irwin Cohen noted that under Greenberg's watch the Indians had several "black players on the major league roster while most clubs in the league still had none."[6]

Greenberg was fired after the 1957 season when the post-Bob Feller era Tribe finished in sixth place. After taking a year away from the game, he rejoined Veeck, who had sold the Indians and bought the White Sox. As vice president and general manager, Greenberg helped assemble the "Go-Go" Sox of 1959, which won the AL pennant before losing in the World Series to the Dodgers, who had migrated to the sunny California coast two years earlier. He left the game for good following the 1961 season and began his "second act" with a career in the investment industry.

Greenberg was inducted into the Baseball Hall of Fame in 1956 in his ninth year of eligibility, receiving 85 percent of the vote (164 of 193 ballots) and becoming the first Jew to be so honored. (He was also installed into the International and National Jewish Sports Halls of Fame in 1979 and 1995, respectively.) His acceptance speech at Cooperstown reflected the immigrant experience, one that might not have been possible had his family wanted to come to the US circa 1938. Speaking on behalf of himself and Joe Cronin, the only other player voted in that year, Greenberg concluded his remarks with thanks and humility.

"[I] want to express my debt to baseball," he said. "It's wonderful to know that a boy from the Bronx of New York who was adept with a baseball bat can win acclaim, reputation, and fame. And it must be a wonderful country if this is possible that it could happen to a boy from the Bronx and a boy from San Francisco."[7]

Greenberg passed away in 1986 at the age of seventy-five after a battle with cancer. The more thoughtful (or morbid) among us might wonder, how will we be remembered when we're gone? What's the first thing people will recall? What would journalists write about Hammerin' Hank, those who had seen this symbolic hero play or had the privilege of knowing him personally, as did Ira Berkow, who took on the solemn task of crafting his memoirs upon Greenberg's request? Or those who had just read the stories or heard them passed down by older relatives?

In Greenberg's case, there were those writers who concentrated on his statistics. But there were also a handful who focused on the man, the sacrifices he made serving during the war, and the abuse he took because of his religious background.

For some, it might have been a special encounter they had with Greenberg. Elliot Denham, a writer for the *Asbury Park Press*, began his column, "The really unforgettable thing about Henry Benjamin "Hank" Greenberg was the handshake."[8] Jim Murray, the Spink Award–winning writer for the *LA Times*, commiserated with Syd Dorfman, a legend in New Jersey sports journalism, noting that "I don't know where he is, or even, for that matter, who he is, but I know that Mr. Dorfman, God bless him, has got to be a sad man today," expressing what many of Greenberg's fans must have felt, especially those who, like Dorfman, were Jewish.[9]

Berkow made Greenberg the subject of his "Sports of the Times" column in the September 7 *New York Times*.

> I never saw Hank Greenberg play, but he was a legendary ballplayer to many, especially in Jewish households, like mine. He was the first truly great Jewish ballplayer and, ironically, a power hitter in the 1930s when the position of Jews in the world—especially, of course, in Hitler's Germany—grew weaker.

Time is a funny thing. As Jews have assimilated into American society in the years since Greenberg faced anti-Semitism on a regular basis, the temporal distance has reduced the effect of his Yom Kippur decision. Sandy Koufax became that symbol for a new generation.

Unlike Greenberg, Koufax did not grow up in an observant Jewish household. Yet he still found it important to refrain from playing on the Day of Atonement, regardless that it meant giving up his starting assignment in the opening game of the 1965 World Series against the Minnesota Twins. (Don Drysdale filled in and was shelled. When manager Walt Alston came to take him out of the game, Drysdale supposedly said, "I bet you wish *I* was Jewish right about now.") Now, whenever the holiday occurs during the baseball season—and to a much lesser extent for football (basketball and hockey begin well after the High Holy Days)—Jewish fans will look at a handful of their *landsmen* major leaguers and wonder if they will make that same choices as Greenberg and Koufax.

Back to Berkow: "Greenberg said he tied to carry himself with dignity because he understood he was a symbol for many Jews in America . . .

"Hank Greenberg was a special man in a special time," Berkow's tribute continued, "He would have been a special man in any time."[10]

Take that, Hitler.

Notes

1 "Hank Greenberg a Hero to Dodgers' Negro Star." *The New York Times*, May 18, 1947.

2 *Hero of Heroes*, p. 65.

3 *Story of My Life*, p. 190.

4 Ibid, p. 191.

5 *The New York Times*, May 18, 1947.

6 Irwin Cohen, "Saluting Satchel and Hank." *Jewish Press*, July 5, 2006.

7 Hank Greenberg's Hall of Fame Induction speech, 1956.

8 "Greenberg Worked for His Fame." *Asbury Park Press*, September 11, 1986.

9 "Upstaged but Never Outplayed." *Los Angeles Times*, September 9, 1986.

10 Ira Berkow, "Greenberg: A Kind of Beacon." *The New York Times*, September 7, 1986.

APPENDIX

Greenberg's 1938 Game Log

Game	Date		Opp	Result	Inngs	PA	AB	R	H
1	Tuesday, April 19	@	CHW	L, 3–4	CG	4	3	1	1
2	Wednesday, April 20	@	CHW	L, 4–5	CG	5	3	1	0
3	Thursday, April 21	@	CHW	W, 9–3	CG	5	3	1	2
4	Friday, April 22		CLE	L, 3–4	CG	4	4	1	1
5	Saturday, April 23		CLE	L, 3–6	CG	5	5	0	0
6	Sunday, April 24		CLE	L, 4–9	CG	4	4	0	0
7	Monday, April 25	@	SLB	W, 10–1	CG	5	3	2	2
8	Tuesday, April 26	@	SLB	W, 7–1	CG	5	5	1	1
9	Wednesday, April 27	@	SLB	L, 2–7	CG	4	3	0	0
10	Friday, April 29		CHW	W, 5–1	CG	5	3	1	1
11	Saturday, April 30	@	CLE	W, 5–3	CG	4	3	1	1
12	Sunday, May 1	@	CLE	L, 3–4	CG	5	5	0	1
13	Monday, May 2	@	CLE	L, 3–11	CG	4	3	0	1
14	Tuesday, May 3	@	BOS	L, 3–4	CG(10)	5	3	1	1
15	Wednesday, May 4	@	BOS	W, 4–1	CG	5	5	1	3
16	Thursday, May 5	@	BOS	W, 7–5	CG	5	5	2	3
17	Saturday, May 7	@	NYY	L, 8–12	CG	5	3	0	0

B	3B	HR	RBI	BB	SO	HBP	SB	CS	BA	OBP	SLG	OPS	BOP
	0	1	1	1	0	0	0	0	.333	.500	1.333	1.833	4
	0	0	0	2	1	0	0	0	.167	.444	.667	1.111	4
	0	1	1	2	0	0	0	0	.333	.571	1.000	1.571	4
	1	0	0	0	1	0	0	0	.308	.500	.923	1.423	4
	0	0	0	0	2	0	0	0	.222	.391	.667	1.058	4
	0	0	0	0	2	0	0	0	.182	.333	.545	.879	4
	0	1	1	2	0	0	0	0	.240	.406	.680	1.086	4
	0	0	1	0	2	0	0	0	.233	.378	.600	.978	4
	0	0	0	1	1	0	0	0	.212	.366	.545	.911	4
	0	0	0	2	0	0	0	0	.222	.391	.556	.947	4
	0	0	0	1	0	0	0	0	.231	.400	.538	.938	4
	0	0	0	0	2	0	1	0	.227	.382	.523	.905	4
	0	0	0	1	0	0	0	0	.234	.390	.511	.900	4
	0	1	1	2	0	0	0	0	.240	.406	.560	.966	4
	0	0	1	0	2	0	0	0	.273	.420	.600	1.020	4
	0	1	1	0	1	0	0	1	.300	.432	.650	1.082	4
	0	0	0	2	0	0	0	0	.286	.430	.619	1.049	4

HANK GREENBERG IN 1938

Game	Date		Opp	Result	Inngs	PA	AB	R	H
18	Sunday, May 8	@	PHA	L, 6–7	CG(10)	5	5	2	2
19	Wednesday, May 11	@	WSH	W, 4–1	CG	5	3	0	1
20	Thursday, May 12	@	WSH	L, 6–7	CG	4	3	1	1
21	Friday, May 13		SLB	W, 7–5	CG	5	4	1	0
22	Sunday, May 15		SLB	L, 1–4	CG(5)	3	2	0	0
23	Monday, May 16		WSH	W, 13–7	CG	5	4	0	2
24	Wednesday, May 18		WSH	L, 1–5	CG	4	3	0	0
25	Thursday, May 19		PHA	W, 6–2	CG	4	2	1	1
26	Friday, May 20		PHA	L, 2–5	CG	4	3	0	1
27	Saturday, May 21		PHA	W, 7–5	CG	4	3	2	1
28	Sunday, May 22		BOS	W, 4–3	CG	4	3	0	1
29	Tuesday, May 24		BOS	L, 4–5	CG	5	3	0	0
30	Wednesday, May 25		NYY	W, 7–3	CG	4	4	2	4
31	Thursday, May 26		NYY	L, 1–5	CG	4	4	0	2
32	Friday, May 27	@	CHW	W, 5–2	CG	4	4	2	3
33	Saturday, May 28	@	CHW	W, 9–1	CG(6)	4	2	2	0
34	Sunday, May 29	@	CHW	W, 2–1	CG	5	3	0	0
35	Monday, May 30 (Game 1)		SLB	W, 10–9	CG	5	5	1	1

B	3B	HR	RBI	BB	SO	HBP	SB	CS	BA	OBP	SLG	OPS	BOP
1	1	1	0	1	0	0	0	.294	.429	.676	1.105	4
0	0	1	2	1	0	0	0	.296	.438	.676	1.114	4
0	1	3	1	0	0	0	0	.297	.441	.703	1.144	4
0	0	0	1	1	0	0	0	.282	.429	.667	1.095	4
0	0	0	1	0	0	0	0	.275	.426	.650	1.076	4
0	0	2	1	1	0	0	0	.286	.434	.643	1.077	4
0	0	0	1	0	0	0	0	.276	.427	.621	1.048	4
0	1	2	2	0	0	1	0	.281	.439	.652	1.090	6
0	0	0	1	0	0	0	1	.283	.441	.641	1.082	6
0	0	0	1	0	0	0	0	.284	.443	.632	1.074	6
0	0	0	1	2	0	0	0	.286	.444	.622	1.067	6
0	0	0	2	0	0	0	0	.277	.443	.604	1.047	6
0	2	2	0	0	0	0	0	.305	.459	.686	1.145	6
0	0	1	0	0	0	0	0	.312	.460	.679	1.139	6
0	1	1	0	0	0	0	0	.327	.469	.708	1.176	4
0	0	1	2	0	0	0	0	.322	.469	.696	1.165	4
0	0	0	2	0	0	0	0	.314	.467	.678	1.145	4
0	1	1	0	2	0	0	0	.309	.459	.683	1.142	4

HANK GREENBERG IN 1938

Game	Date		Opp	Result	Inngs	PA	AB	R	H
36	Monday, May 30 (Game 2)		SLB	L, 0–3	CG	4	4	0	2
37	Wednesday, June 1	@	NYY	W, 8–4	CG	5	5	3	3
38	Thursday, June 2 (Game 1)	@	NYY	L, 4–5	CG	4	3	0	0
39	Thursday, June 2 (Game 2)	@	NYY	L, 2–5	CG	4	4	0	1
40	Friday, June 3	@	NYY	L, 1–5	CG	4	4	0	1
41	Saturday, June 4	@	BOS	L, 3–5	CG	4	4	0	0
42	Sunday, June 5	@	BOS	W, 10–4	CG	5	3	1	1
43	Monday, June 6	@	BOS	L, 7–8	CG	4	4	1	1
44	Tuesday, June 7	@	PHA	W, 5–4	CG	4	4	0	0
45	Wednesday, June 8	@	PHA	W, 5–1	CG	4	4	0	0
46	Thursday, June 9	@	PHA	L, 5–8	CG	5	4	1	2
47	Friday, June 10	@	WSH	W, 7–6	CG(10)	5	5	1	1
48	Saturday, June 11	@	WSH	W, 7–2	CG	4	3	0	0
49	Sunday, June 12	@	WSH	W, 18–12	CG	6	4	4	2
50	Tuesday, June 14		PHA	L, 2–8	CG	4	4	1	1
51	Wednesday, June 15		PHA	L, 6–7	CG	5	4	1	2
52	Thursday, June 16		PHA	W, 12–3	CG	5	5	3	2

3B	HR	RBI	BB	SO	HBP	SB	CS	BA	OBP	SLG	OPS	BOP
0	0	0	0	0	0	0	0	.315	.460	.677	1.137	4
0	1	1	0	0	0	0	0	.326	.464	.697	1.161	4
0	0	0	0	0	1	0	0	.319	.459	.681	1.140	4
0	0	1	0	2	0	0	0	.317	.454	.676	1.130	4
0	0	0	0	0	0	0	0	.315	.449	.664	1.114	4
0	0	0	0	0	0	0	0	.306	.440	.646	1.086	4
0	0	0	2	1	0	1	0	.307	.444	.640	1.084	4
1	0	1	0	0	0	0	0	.305	.440	.643	1.083	4
0	0	0	0	1	0	0	0	.297	.431	.627	1.057	4
0	0	1	0	1	0	0	0	.290	.422	.611	1.033	4
0	0	1	1	2	0	0	1	.295	.426	.608	1.035	4
0	0	0	0	1	0	0	0	.292	.421	.602	1.023	4
0	0	0	1	1	0	0	0	.287	.418	.592	1.010	4
1	0	2	2	0	0	0	0	.292	.425	.601	1.026	4
0	1	2	0	1	0	0	0	.291	.422	.610	1.031	4
0	0	0	1	1	0	0	0	.296	.425	.608	1.033	4
0	0	0	0	0	0	0	0	.298	.425	.602	1.027	6

HANK GREENBERG IN 1938

Game	Date		Opp	Result	Inngs	PA	AB	R	H
53	Friday, June 17 (Game 1)		WSH	L, 10–12	CG	5	4	1	0
54	Friday, June 17 (Game 2)		WSH	W, 4–3	CG	4	4	2	3
55	Saturday, June 18		WSH	W, 5–3	CG	4	4	1	2
56	Sunday, June 19		WSH	L, 6–10	CG	4	2	1	1
57	Monday, June 21 (Game 1)		BOS	L, 3–8	CG	4	4	0	0
58	Monday, June 21 (Game 2)		BOS	W, 5–4	CG	4	3	0	0
59	Wednesday, June 22		BOS	W, 8–3	CG	4	3	1	1
60	Thursday, June 23		BOS	W, 10–2	CG	5	3	1	1
61	Friday, June 24		NYY	W, 12–8	CG	5	2	4	2
62	Saturday, June 25		NYY	L, 3–9	CG	4	3	0	0
63	Sunday, June 26		NYY	L, 3–10	CG	4	3	0	0
64	Tuesday, June 28	@	CLE	L, 4–5	CG	4	3	0	0
65	Wednesday, June 29	@	CLE	W, 4–3	CG	4	4	1	1
66	Thursday, June 30	@	CLE	L, 9–10	CG	5	4	1	2
67	Saturday, July 2	@	SLB	L, 5–13	CG	4	3	1	1
68	Sunday, July 3 (Game 1)	@	SLB	L, 5–6	CG(10)	4	4	0	1
69	Sunday, July 3 (Game 2)	@	SLB	L, 2–6	CG	4	4	1	1
70	Monday, July 4 Game (1)		CLE	W, 7–3	CG	5	3	1	1

B	3B	HR	RBI	BB	SO	HBP	SB	CS	BA	OBP	SLG	OPS	BOP
0	0	0	0	1	1	0	0	0	.292	.420	.590	1.010	6
0	0	1	1	0	1	0	0	0	.302	.426	.608	1.034	6
0	0	1	1	0	1	0	0	1	.305	.427	.621	1.048	6
0	0	0	0	2	0	0	0	0	.307	.432	.620	1.052	6
0	0	0	0	0	1	0	0	0	.301	.425	.608	1.033	6
0	0	0	0	1	1	0	0	0	.297	.422	.599	1.022	6
0	0	1	3	1	1	0	0	0	.298	.424	.609	1.033	6
0	0	1	1	1	0	0	0	0	.298	.425	.619	1.044	6
0	0	2	5	3	0	0	0	0	.305	.435	.650	1.085	6
0	0	0	0	1	0	0	0	0	.300	.433	.641	1.074	6
0	0	0	0	1	1	0	0	0	.296	.430	.633	1.063	6
0	0	0	0	1	0	0	0	0	.293	.428	.624	1.052	6
0	0	1	3	0	0	0	0	0	.292	.425	.631	1.056	5
0	0	1	2	1	0	0	0	0	.295	.428	.641	1.069	5
0	0	0	0	1	0	0	0	0	.296	.429	.638	1.067	5
0	0	0	1	0	0	0	0	0	.295	.427	.631	1.058	5
0	0	0	0	0	1	0	0	0	.294	.424	.625	1.049	5
0	0	0	0	2	1	0	0	0	.295	.427	.622	1.049	5

HANK GREENBERG IN 1938

Game	Date		Opp	Result	Inngs	PA	AB	R	H
71	Monday, July 4 Game (2)		CLE	W, 5–2	CG	4	4	1	1
72	Friday, July 8 (Game 1)		CHW	W, 7–5	CG	4	3	3	2
73	Friday, July 8 (Game 2)		CHW	L, 3–5	CG(11)	5	4	0	1
74	Saturday, July 9		CHW	W, 4–0	CG	4	3	2	3
75	Sunday, July 10		CHW	L, 4–5	CG	4	3	2	2
76	Wednesday, July 13 (Game 1)	@	BOS	L, 4–7	CG	4	4	0	1
77	Wednesday, July 13 (Game 2)	@	BOS	W, 9–5	CG	5	4	2	1
78	Thursday, July 14	@	BOS	L, 1–12	CG	4	4	0	0
79	Friday, July 15	@	NYY	L, 0–3	CG(6)	2	2	0	0
80	Saturday, July 16	@	NYY	L, 5–7	CG	5	4	2	1
81	Sunday, July 17	@	NYY	L, 3–16	CG	4	4	1	2
82	Tuesday, July 19	@	WSH	L, 3–4	CG(10)	5	4	0	1
83	Wednesday, July 20	@	WSH	L, 2–7	CG	4	4	0	0
84	Thursday, July 21	@	WSH	L, 3–4	CG	4	4	0	1
85	Sunday, July 24 (Game 1)	@	PHA	W, 7–6	CG	4	4	2	2
86	Sunday, July 24 (Game 2)	@	PHA	W, 7–3	CG	5	4	0	1
87	Tuesday, July 26		WSH	W, 6–5	CG	4	3	2	2
88	Wednesday, July 27		WSH	W, 9–4	CG	4	3	2	2

3B	HR	RBI	BB	SO	HBP	SB	CS	BA	OBP	SLG	OPS	BOP
0	0	0	0	2	0	0	0	.294	.425	.620	1.045	5
0	1	1	1	0	0	0	0	.298	.429	.632	1.061	5
0	0	0	1	1	0	1	0	.298	.429	.626	1.055	5
0	2	3	1	0	0	0	0	.306	.436	.653	1.088	5
0	1	2	1	0	0	1	0	.310	.439	.664	1.104	5
0	0	1	0	0	0	0	1	.309	.437	.658	1.095	5
0	0	0	1	1	0	0	0	.308	.437	.656	1.092	5
0	0	0	0	1	0	0	0	.304	.431	.646	1.078	5
0	0	0	0	0	0	0	0	.301	.429	.642	1.071	5
0	1	1	1	0	0	0	0	.301	.429	.647	1.075	5
0	1	2	0	0	0	0	0	.303	.429	.655	1.085	5
0	0	0	1	1	0	0	0	.303	.429	.650	1.079	4
0	0	0	0	0	0	0	0	.299	.424	.641	1.065	4
0	0	0	0	1	0	0	0	.298	.422	.636	1.058	4
0	1	4	0	1	0	0	0	.301	.423	.644	1.067	4
0	0	0	1	0	0	0	0	.300	.423	.639	1.062	4
0	2	2	0	0	0	0	0	.304	.425	.658	1.083	4
0	2	5	1	0	0	0	0	.307	.428	.677	1.105	4

HANK GREENBERG IN 1938

Game	Date		Opp	Result	Inngs	PA	AB	R	H
89	Thursday, July 28		WSH	W, 12–4	CG	5	4	0	1
90	Friday, July 29		PHA	W, 9–2	CG	4	4	3	3
91	Saturday, July 30 (Game 1)		PHA	W, 10–7	CG	5	3	1	2
92	Saturday, July 30 (Game 2)		PHA	W, 8–7	CG	5	4	1	1
93	Monday, August 1		PHA	L, 0–4	CG	5	4	0	1
94	Tuesday, August 2		NYY	W, 4–3	CG	4	4	0	1
95	Wednesday, August 3		NYY	L, 7–10	CG(11)	6	5	3	3
96	Thursday, August 4		NYY	L, 4–8	CG	4	4	1	1
97	Friday, August 5		BOS	L, 8–9	CG(10)	5	2	1	0
98	Saturday, August 6		BOS	L, 8–14	CG	5	4	1	2
99	Sunday, August 7		BOS	W, 7–3	CG	4	3	1	1
100	Tuesday, August 9	@	CHW	W, 4–1	CG	4	2	2	2
101	Wednesday, August 10	@	CHW	L, 7–8	CG	5	5	1	2
102	Thursday, August 11	@	CHW	L, 1–13	CG	4	3	0	0
103	Saturday, August 13	@	SLB	L, 3–6	CG	4	4	0	1
104	Sunday, August 14 (Game 1)	@	SLB	L, 1–7	CG	4	4	0	0
105	Sunday, August 14 (Game 2)	@	SLB	T, 3–3	CG	4	4	0	0

3	3B	HR	RBI	BB	SO	HBP	SB	CS	BA	OBP	SLG	OPS	BOP
	0	0	1	1	0	0	0	0	.306	.428	.675	1.103	4
	0	2	4	0	0	0	0	0	.312	.431	.698	1.129	4
	0	1	3	2	1	0	0	0	.315	.436	.706	1.142	4
	0	1	2	1	1	0	0	0	.314	.435	.710	1.145	4
	0	0	0	1	0	0	0	0	.313	.435	.704	1.139	4
	0	0	0	0	2	0	0	0	.313	.433	.702	1.135	4
	0	0	1	1	1	0	0	0	.317	.436	.701	1.137	4
	0	0	0	0	1	0	0	0	.316	.435	.695	1.130	4
	0	0	0	3	0	0	0	0	.314	.437	.691	1.128	4
	0	0	3	1	0	0	0	0	.316	.439	.692	1.131	4
	0	1	3	1	2	0	0	0	.317	.439	.697	1.137	4
	0	0	0	2	0	0	0	0	.320	.444	.699	1.143	4
	0	0	0	0	0	0	0	0	.321	.444	.695	1.139	4
	0	0	1	1	2	0	0	0	.319	.442	.689	1.131	4
	0	0	0	0	0	0	0	0	.318	.440	.685	1.125	4
	0	0	0	0	4	0	0	0	.315	.436	.677	1.114	4
	0	0	0	0	0	0	0	0	.311	.433	.670	1.103	4

HANK GREENBERG IN 1938

Game	Date		Opp	Result	Inngs	PA	AB	R	H
106	Wednesday, August 17 (Game 1)		CHW	W, 4–3	CG	4	4	0	0
107	Wednesday, August 17 (Game 2)		CHW	W, 3–2	CG	4	4	0	0
108	Thursday, August 18		CHW	W, 5–1	CG	5	4	0	2
109	Friday, August 19 (Game 1)		SLB	W, 8–7	CG	5	5	2	2
110	Friday, August 19 (Game 2)		SLB	W, 7–4	CG	4	2	1	2
111	Saturday, August 20		SLB	W, 6–4	CG	4	3	1	0
112	Sunday, August 21		SLB	L, 4–9	CG	5	4	1	1
113	Tuesday, August 23 (Game 1)	@	PHA	W, 13–5	GS-7	4	3	2	1
114	Tuesday, August 23 (Game 2)	@	PHA	W, 8–3	CG	5	5	2	2
115	Wednesday, August 24 (Game 1)	@	PHA	L, 5–10	CG	5	4	0	1
116	Wednesday, August 24 (Game 2)	@	PHA	L, 2–11	CG	4	4	0	0
117	Thursday, August 25	@	WSH	L, 2–8	CG	4	2	0	0
118	Friday, August 26	@	WSH	W, 9–3	CG	5	4	1	1
119	Saturday, August 27	@	WSH	W, 12–11	CG	5	4	1	1
120	Sunday, August 28	@	BOS	W, 4–3	CG(10)	4	4	1	1

B	3B	HR	RBI	BB	SO	HBP	SB	CS	BA	OBP	SLG	OPS	BOP
	0	0	0	0	0	0	0	0	.308	.429	.663	1.092	4
	0	0	0	0	0	0	0	0	.305	.425	.656	1.082	4
	0	0	3	0	1	0	0	0	.307	.426	.655	1.081	4
	0	2	5	0	0	0	0	0	.308	.426	.667	1.092	4
	0	1	3	2	0	0	0	0	.312	.430	.676	1.106	4
	0	0	0	1	1	0	0	0	.309	.429	.671	1.100	4
	0	1	2	1	0	0	1	0	.309	.429	.674	1.103	4
	0	0	1	0	2	1	0	0	.309	.429	.674	1.103	4
	0	1	2	0	0	0	0	0	.310	.429	.680	1.109	6
	0	0	1	1	0	0	0	0	.309	.429	.676	1.105	4
	0	0	1	0	1	0	0	0	.306	.425	.670	1.095	4
	0	0	0	2	0	0	0	0	.305	.426	.667	1.092	4
	0	0	2	1	1	0	0	0	.304	.426	.663	1.088	4
	0	1	1	1	0	0	0	0	.304	.425	.666	1.091	4
	0	1	1	0	0	0	0	0	.303	.424	.669	1.093	4

HANK GREENBERG IN 1938

Game	Date		Opp	Result	Inngs	PA	AB	R	H
121	Monday, August 29	@	BOS	W, 15–1	CG	6	3	2	0
122	Tuesday, August 30	@	NYY	L, 1–3	CG	4	4	0	2
123	Wednesday, August 31	@	NYY	W, 12–6	CG	5	5	2	3
124	Thursday, September 1	@	NYY	W, 6–3	CG	5	5	1	2
125	Saturday, September 3	@	CHW	W, 11–4	CG	5	2	3	1
126	Sunday, September 4	@	CHW	L, 1–2	CG(10)	4	2	0	0
127	Monday, september 5 (Game 1)	@	SLB	L, 2–3	CG	4	1	1	0
128	Monday, september 5 (Game 2)	@	SLB	W, 9–3	CG(6)	4	3	1	0
129	Tuesday, September 6		CLE	L, 0–6	CG	4	4	0	1
130	Wednesday, September 7		CLE	L, 0–1	CG	4	3	0	0
131	Thursday, September 8	@	CLE	W, 4–1	CG	5	4	0	1
132	Friday, September 9	@	CLE	W, 11–5	CG	5	5	2	2
133	Sunday, September 11 (Game 1)		CHW	W, 10–1	CG	5	5	2	2
134	Sunday, September 11 (Game 2)		CHW	W, 5–3	CG	4	2	1	1
135	Monday, September 12		CHW	W, 4–3	CG	4	3	3	1
136	Tuesday, September 13		BOS	W, 9–3	CG	5	3	1	1

B	3B	HR	RBI	BB	SO	HBP	SB	CS	BA	OBP	SLG	OPS	BOP
	0	0	0	2	1	1	0	0	.301	.425	.664	1.089	4
	0	0	1	0	1	0	0	0	.303	.425	.663	1.088	4
	0	1	3	0	0	0	0	0	.306	.427	.673	1.100	4
	0	0	1	0	2	0	0	0	.308	.427	.673	1.099	4
	0	0	0	3	1	0	0	0	.308	.430	.672	1.102	4
	0	0	0	2	2	0	0	0	.307	.431	.669	1.099	4
	0	0	0	3	0	0	0	0	.306	.433	.667	1.100	4
	0	0	0	1	0	0	0	0	.304	.432	.663	1.095	4
	0	0	0	0	0	0	0	0	.304	.430	.659	1.090	4
	0	0	0	1	1	0	0	0	.302	.429	.655	1.084	4
	0	0	1	1	1	0	0	0	.301	.429	.654	1.083	4
	0	1	3	0	2	0	0	0	.303	.429	.658	1.086	4
	0	2	4	0	0	0	0	0	.304	.428	.667	1.096	4
	0	0	1	2	0	0	0	0	.304	.431	.667	1.097	4
	0	1	1	1	0	0	0	0	.305	.431	.671	1.102	4
	0	0	1	2	1	0	0	0	.305	.432	.669	1.101	4

HANK GREENBERG IN 1938

Game	Date		Opp	Result	Inngs	PA	AB	R	H
137	Wednesday, September 14		BOS	L, 2–9	CG	4	4	1	1
138	Thursday, September 15		NYY	W, 6–4	CG	4	3	0	0
139	Friday, September 16		NYY	L, 4–6	CG	4	4	2	3
140	Saturday, September 17		NYY	W, 7–3	CG	4	4	2	4
141	Sunday, September 18		WSH	W, 8–1	CG	5	5	1	1
142	Monday, September 19		WSH	L, 2–12	CG	4	3	0	1
143	Wednesday, September 21 (Game 1)		PHA	W, 8–6	CG	5	5	1	3
144	Wednesday, September 21 (Game 2)		PHA	W, 3–0	CG(5)	3	3	0	0
145	Friday, September 23 (Game 1)		CLE	L, 1–8	CG	4	4	0	1
146	Friday, September 23 (Game 2)		CLE	L, 5–6	CG(7)	4	3	2	3
147	Saturday, September 24		CLE	W, 7–6	CG	4	2	1	0
148	Sunday, September 25		CLE	W, 7–5	CG	4	4	1	1
149	Tuesday, September 27 (Game 1)		SLB	W, 5–4	CG	4	1	0	1
150	Tuesday, September 27 (Game 2)		SLB	W, 10–2	CG(7)	4	4	2	2
151	Wednesday, September 28		SLB	W, 12–0	CG	5	3	2	0
152	Thursday, September 29		SLB	W, 6–2	CG	4	4	0	1

B	3B	HR	RBI	BB	SO	HBP	SB	CS	BA	OBP	SLG	OPS	BOP
	0	0	0	0	0	0	0	0	.304	.431	.667	1.099	4
	0	0	0	1	1	0	0	0	.302	.430	.663	1.093	4
	0	1	1	0	1	0	0	0	.306	.432	.670	1.102	4
	0	2	5	0	0	0	0	0	.312	.436	.685	1.120	4
	0	0	1	0	1	0	0	0	.310	.434	.680	1.114	4
	0	0	0	1	0	0	0	0	.311	.434	.678	1.112	4
	0	1	6	0	0	0	0	0	.313	.436	.683	1.118	4
	0	0	0	0	1	0	0	0	.312	.434	.679	1.112	4
	0	0	0	0	0	0	0	0	.311	.432	.676	1.108	4
	0	2	2	1	0	0	0	0	.315	.436	.689	1.125	4
	0	0	0	2	0	0	0	0	.314	.436	.686	1.123	4
	0	0	1	0	1	0	0	0	.313	.435	.685	1.120	4
	0	0	1	3	0	0	0	0	.315	.439	.685	1.124	4
	0	2	4	0	0	0	0	0	.316	.439	.695	1.134	4
	0	0	0	2	2	0	1	0	.314	.439	.691	1.130	4
	0	0	0	0	0	0	0	0	.314	.438	.688	1.126	4

HANK GREENBERG IN 1938

Game	Date		Opp	Result	Inngs	PA	AB	R	H
153	Saturday, October 1	@	CLE	L, 0–5	CG	4	4	0	0
154	Sunday, October 2 (Game 1)	@	CLE	W, 4–1	CG	5	4	2	1
155	Sunday, October 2 (Game 2)	@	CLE	W, 10–8	CG(7)	4	3	3	3
	TOTALS					681	556	143	175

Key
Opp   Opponent
Inngs   Innings
CG   Complete Game
PA   Plate Appearances
AB   At-Bats
R   Runs
H   Hits
2B   Doubles
3B   Triples
HR   Home Runs
RBI   Runs Batted In
BB   Base on Balls
SO   Strikeout
HBP   Hit by Pitch
SB   Stolen Bases
CS   Caught Stealing
BA   Batting Average
OBP   On-Base Percentage
SLG   Slugging
OPS   On Base + Slugging
BOP   Batting Order Place

B	3B	HR	RBI	BB	SO	HBP	SB	CS	BA	OBP	SLG	OPS	BOP
	0	0	0	0	1	0	0	0	.311	.435	.683	1.118	4
	0	0	0	1	2	0	0	0	.311	.435	.682	1.116	4
	0	0	1	1	0	0	0	0	.315	.438	.683	1.122	4
3	4	58	147	119	92	3	7	5	.315	.438	.683	1.122	

Greenberg's Walks, September 1938

Date	Opponent	Greenberg Walks	Pitcher (Status)	Greenberg Walks/ Total Walks	Pitcher w/9 IP in 1938	Notes
September 3	Chicago	3	Jack Knott (V)	2/2	3.7	
			Harry Boyles (R)	1/1	7.7	
September 4	Chicago	2	Johnny Rigney (V)	2/4	3.9	Sophomore season
September 5	St. Louis	3	Lefty Mills (R)	3/6	5	1st game of doubleheader
September 5	St. Louis	1	Bobo Newsom (V)	1/5	5.2	2nd game of doubleheader
September 7	Cleveland	1	Mel Harder (V)	1/3	2.3	
September 8	Cleveland	1	Earl Whitehill (V)	1/5	4.7	
September 11	Chicago	2	Johnny Rigney (V)	2/6	3.9	2nd game of doubleheader
September 12	Chicago	1	Jack Knott (V)	1/2	3.7	
September 13*	Boston	2	Bill Harris (V)	/1	2.4	Final season in career
			Jim Bagby (R)	1/1	4.1	
			Dick Midkiff (R)	/4	5.3	Only season in Majors
			Ted Olson	0	3.9	
September 15	New York	1	Bump Hadley (V)	1/4	3.5	
September 19	Washington	1	Pete Appleton (V)	1/7	3.3	
September 23*	Cleveland	1	Earl Whitehill (V)	/3	4.7	2nd game of doubleheader, 7 innings
			Johnny Humphries (R)	/2	5.5	
September 24	Cleveland	2	Mel Harder (V)	2/4	2.3	
			Al Milnar (R)	0/1	3.4	
			Willis Hudlin (V)	0/1	3.2	

Date	Opponent	Greenberg Walks	Pitcher (Status)	Greenberg Walks/ Total Walks	Pitcher w/9 IP in 1938	Notes
eptember 27 *	St. Louis	3	Jim Walkup (V)	/5	5.1	1st games of doubleheader 1–12 record
			Fred Johnson (R)	/2	3.5	1st game. 44 years old; absence of 15 seasons (1923-38)
eptember 28 *	St. Louis	2	Lefty Mills (R)	/5	5	
			Emil Bildilli (R)	/2	4.6	Nickname: "Hill Billy"
)ctober 2	Cleveland	1	Bob Feller (V)	1/7	6.7	19 years old; 1st game of doubleheader
)ctober 2 *	Cleveland	1	Johnny Humphries (R)	/2	5.5	2nd game of doubleheader, 7 innings
			Clay Smith (R)	/1	4.1	

Exact walk breakdown unavailable.

/: Veteran

R: Rookie

League Average: 3.7

Greenberg Gets a Free Pass

Month	Games	Walks		September vs. Team	
April	11	11		St. Louis	9
May	25	23		Chicago	8
June	30	20		Cleveland	7
July	26	16		Boston	2
August	31	21		New York	1
Sept/Oct	32	28		Washington	1
	155	**119**		Philadelphia	0
					28

	Games	Walks
First Half	71	57
Second Half	84	62

Greenberg's Home Runs and Splits, 1938

HR#	Date	Opponent		Pitcher	Inning	RBI
1	4/19	@	CHW	John Whitehead	t 5	1
2	4/21	@	CHW	Bill Dietrich	t 6	1
3	4/25	@	SLB	Ed Cole	t 3	1
4	5/3	@	BOS	Lefty Grove	t 2	1
5	5/5	@	BOS	Fritz Ostermueller	t 6	1
6	5/8	@	PHA	Lynn Nelson	t 6	1
7	5/12	@	WSH	Pete Appleton	t 8	3
8	5/19		PHA	Lynn Nelson	b 6	2
9	5/25		NYY	Joe Beggs	b 3	1
10	5/25		NYY	Ivy Andrews	b 5	1
11	5/27	@	CHW	Frank Gabler	t 3	1
12	5/30 (1)		SLB	Ed Linke	b 8	1
13	6/1	@	NYY	Bump Hadley	t 9	1
14	6/14		PHA	Lynn Nelson	b 8	2
15	6/17 (2)		WSH	Dutch Leonard	b 7	1
16	6/18		WSH	Jimmie DeShong	b 2	1
17	6/22		BOS	Lefty Grove	b 1	3
18	6/23		BOS	Johnny Marcum	b 2	1
19	6/24		NYY	Spud Chandler	b 3	3
20	6/24		NYY	Steve Sundra	b 8	2
21	6/29	@	CLE	Mel Harder	t 8	3
22	6/30	@	CLE	Bob Feller	t 3	1

HANK GREENBERG IN 1938

HR#	Date	Opponent		Pitcher	Inning	RBI
23	7/9 (1)		CHW	Monty Stratton	b 3	1
24	7/9		CHW	John Whitehead	b 4	1
25	7/9		CHW	John Whitehead	b 7	1
26	7/10		CHW	Ted Lyons	b 8	2
27	7/16	@	NYY	Red Ruffing	t 8	1
28	7/17	@	NYY	Spud Chandler	t 8	1
29	7/24 (1)	@	PHA	Nels Potter	t 5	4
30	7/26		WSH	Wes Ferrell	b 4	1
31	7/26		WSH	Chief Hogsett	b 8	1
32	7/27		WSH	Monte Weaver	b 1	3
33	7/27		WSH	Pete Appleton	b 2	2
34	7/29		PHA	Al Williams	b 4	1
35	7/29		PHA	Nels Potter	b 7	3
36	7/30 (1)		PHA	Bud Thomas	b 8	3
37	7/30 (2)		PHA	George Caster	b 8	2
38	8/7		BOS	Jack Wilson	b 1	3
39	8/19 (1)		SLB	Oral Hildebrand	b 4	4
40	8/19 (1)		SLB	Fred Johnson	b 9	1
41	8/19 (2)		SLB	Lefty Mills	b 1	3
42	8/21		SLB	Bobo Newsom	b 7	1
43	8/23 (2)	@	PHA	Bud Thomas	t 6	1
44	8/27	@	WSH	Ken Chase	t 4	1
45	8/28	@	BOS	Emerson Dickman	t 7	1

HR#	Date	Opponent		Pitcher	Inning	RBI
46	8/31	@	NYY	Steve Sundra	t 2	1
47	9/9	@	CLE	Ken Jungels	t 6	2
48	9/11 (1)		CHW	Ted Lyons	b 3	2
49	9/11 (1)		CHW	Ted Lyons	b 5	1
50	9/12		CHW	Jack Knott	b 3	1
51	9/16		NYY	Lefty Gomez	b 4	1
52	9/17		NYY	Monte Pearson	b 1	2
53	9/17		NYY	Monte Pearson	b 5	3
54	9/21 (1)		PHA	Ralph Buxton	b 1	3
55	9/23 (2)		CLE	Earl Whitehill	b 4	1
56	9/23 (2)		CLE	Earl Whitehill	b 7	1
57	9/27 (2)		SLB	Bill Cox	b 1	2
58	9/27 (2)		SLB	Bill Cox	b 3	2

Vs. RHP	49
Vs. LHP	9

Home	39
Away	19

First Half	(71 games)	22
Second Half	(84 games)	36

Home Runs by Month

April	3
May	9
June	10
July	15
August	9
September	12
October	0

Clutch Stats

Split	G	PA	AB	HR
2 outs RISP	45	56	46	2
Late & Close	30	38	30	2
Tie Game	53	72	59	4
Within 1 R	60	129	104	5
Within 2 R	66	190	159	14
Within 3 R	69	230	191	17
Within 4 R	69	257	217	19
Margin > 4 R	26	56	50	7
Ahead	43	115	96	9
Behind	47	126	112	13

RISP Runners in Scoring Position

Late & Close the seventh inning or later with the batting team ahead by one, tied, or has the tying run on base, at bat, or on deck.

Hank Greenberg, 1938 vs. Babe Ruth, 1927: A Homer-by-Homer Comparison

Hank Greenberg, 1938							
Game No.	HR No.	Date			Pitcher		Inn
1	1	4/19	@	CHW	John Whitehead		t 5
3	2	4/21	@	CHW	Bill Dietrich		t 6
7	3	4/25	@	SLB	Ed Cole		t 3
14	4	5/3	@	BOS	Lefty Grove		t 2
16	5	5/5	@	BOS	Fritz Ostermueller		t 6
18	6	5/8	@	PHA	Lynn Nelson		t 6
20	7	5/12	@	WSH	Pete Appleton		t 8
25	8	5/19		PHA	Lynn Nelson		b 6
30	9	5/25		NYY	Joe Beggs		b 3
30	10	5/25		NYY	Ivy Andrews		b 5
32	11	5/27	@	CHW	Frank Gabler		t 3
35	12	5/30 (Game 1)		SLB	Ed Linke		b 8
37	13	6/1	@	NYY	Bump Hadley		t 9
50	14	6/14		PHA	Lynn Nelson		b 8
54	15	6/17 (Game 2)		WSH	Dutch Leonard		b 7
55	16	6/18		WSH	Jimmie DeShong		b 2
59	17	6/22		BOS	Lefty Grove		b 1
60	18	6/23		BOS	Johnny Marcum		b 2
61	19	6/24		NYY	Spud Chandler		b 3

		Babe Ruth, 1927				
Game No.	HR No.	Date			Pitcher	Inn
4	1	4/15/1927		PHA	Howard Ehmke	b 1
11	2	4/23/1927	@	PHA	Rube Walberg	t 1
12	3	4/24/1927	@	WSH	Sloppy Thurston	t 6
14	4	4/29/1927	@	BOS	Slim Harriss	t 5
16	5	5/1/1927		PHA	Jack Quinn	b 1
16	6	5/1/1927		PHA	Rube Walberg	b 8
24	7	5/10/1927	@	SLB	Milt Gaston	t 1
24	8	5/11/1927	@	SLB	Ernie Nevers	t 1
29	9	5/17/1927	@	DET	Rip Collins	t 8
33	10	5/22/1927	@	CLE	Benn Karr	t 6
34	11	5/23/1927	@	WSH	Sloppy Thurston	t 1
37	12	5/28 (Game 1)		WSH	Sloppy Thurston	b 7
39	13	5/29/1927		BOS	Danny MacFayden	b 8
41	14	5/30 (Game 2)	@	PHA	Rube Walberg	t 11
42	15	5/31 (Game 1)	@	PHA	Jack Quinn	t 1
43	16	5/31 (Game 2)	@	PHA	Howard Ehmke	t 5
47	17	6/5/1927		DET	Earl Whitehill	b 6
48	18	6/7/1927		CHW	Tommy Thomas	b 4
52	19	6/11/1927		CLE	Garland Buckeye	b 3

		Hank Greenberg, 1938				
Game No.	**HR No.**	**Date**			**Pitcher**	**Inn**
61	20	6/24		NYY	Steve Sundra	b 8
65	21	6/29	@	CLE	Mel Harder	t 8
66	22	6/30	@	CLE	Bob Feller	t 3
72	23	7/08 (Game 1)		CHW	Monty Stratton	b 3
74	24	7/9		CHW	John Whitehead	b 4
74	25	7/9		CHW	John Whitehead	b 7
75	26	7/10		CHW	Ted Lyons	b 8
80	27	7/16	@	NYY	Red Ruffing	t 8
81	28	7/17	@	NYY	Spud Chandler	t 8
85	29	7/24 (Game 1)	@	PHA	Nels Potter	t 5
87	30	7/26		WSH	Wes Ferrell	b 4
87	31	7/26		WSH	Chief Hogsett	b 8
88	32	7/27		WSH	Monte Weaver	b 1
88	33	7/27		WSH	Pete Appleton	b 2
90	34	7/29		PHA	Al Williams	b 4
90	35	7/29		PHA	Nels Potter	b 7
91	36	7/30 (Game 1)		PHA	Bud Thomas	b 8
92	37	7/30 (Game 2)		PHA	George Caster	b 8
99	38	8/7		BOS	Jack Wilson	b 1
109	39	8/19 (Game 1)		SLB	Oral Hildebrand	b 4
109	40	8/19 (Game 1)		SLB	Fred Johnson	b 9
110	41	8/19 (Game 2)		SLB	Lefty Mills	b 1

Babe Ruth, 1927						
Game No.	HR No.	Date			Pitcher	Inn
52	20	6/11/1927		CLE	Garland Buckeye	b 5
53	21	6/12/1927		CLE	George Uhle	b 7
55	22	6/16/1927		SLB	Tom Zachary	b 1
60	23	6/22 (Game 1)	@	BOS	Hooks Wiltse	t 5
60	24	6/22 (Game 1)	@	BOS	Hooks Wiltse	t 7
66/70	25	6/30/1927		BOS	Slim Harriss	b 4
69/73	26	7/3/1927	@	WSH	Hod Lisenbee	t 1
74/78	27	7/8 (Game 2)	@	DET	Don Hankins	t 2
75/79	28	7/9 (Game 1)	@	DET	Ken Holloway	t 1
75/79	29	7/9 (Game 1)	@	DET	Ken Holloway	t 4
79/83	30	7/12/1927	@	CLE	Joe Shaute	t 9
90/94	31	7/24/1927	@	CHW	Tommy Thomas	t 3
91/95	32	7/26 (Game 1)		SLB	Milt Gaston	b 1
91/95	33	7/26 (Game 1)		SLB	Milt Gaston	b 6
94/98	34	7/28/1927		SLB	Lefty Stewart	b 8
102/106	35	8/5/1927		DET	George Smith	b 8
106/110	36	8/10/1927	@	WSH	Tom Zachary	t 3
110/114	37	8/16/1927	@	CHW	Tommy Thomas	t 5
111/115	38	8/17/1927	@	CHW	Sarge Connally	t 11
114/118	39	8/20/1927	@	CLE	Jake Miller	t 1
116/120	40	8/22/1927	@	CLE	Joe Shaute	t 6
120/124	41	8/27/1927	@	SLB	Ernie Nevers	t 8

Hank Greenberg, 1938						
Game No.	HR No.	Date			Pitcher	Inn
112	42	8/21		SLB	Bobo Newsom	b 7
114	43	8/23 (Game 2)	@	PHA	Bud Thomas	t 6
119	44	8/27	@	WSH	Ken Chase	t 4
120	45	8/28	@	BOS	Emerson Dickman	t 7
123	46	8/31	@	NYY	Steve Sundra	t 2
132	47	9/9	@	CLE	Ken Jungels	t 6
133	48	9/11 (Game1)		CHW	Ted Lyons	b 3
133	49	9/11 (Game1)		CHW	Ted Lyons	b 5
135	50	9/12		CHW	Jack Knott	b 3
139	51	9/16		NYY	Lefty Gomez	b 4
140	52	9/17		NYY	Monte Pearson	b 1
140	53	9/17		NYY	Monte Pearson	b 5
143	54	9/21 (Game 1)		PHA	Ralph Buxton	b 1
146	55	9/23 (Game 2)		CLE	Earl Whitehill	b 4
146	56	9/23 (Game 2)		CLE	Earl Whitehill	b 7
150	57	9/27 (Game 2)		SLB	Bill Cox	b 1
150	58	9/27 (Game 2)		SLB	Bill Cox	b 3

Babe Ruth, 1927							
Game No.	**HR No.**	**Date**			**Pitcher**	**Inn**	
121/125	42	8/28/1927	@	SLB	Ernie Wingard	t 1	
123/127	43	8/31/1927		BOS	Tony Welzer	b 8	
124/128	44	9/2/1927	@	PHA	Rube Walberg	t 1	
128/132	45	9/6 (Game 1)	@	BOS	Tony Welzer	t 6	
128/132	46	9/6 (Game 1)	@	BOS	Tony Welzer	t 7	
129/133	47	9/6 (Game 2)	@	BOS	Jack Russell	t 9	
130/134	48	9/7/1927	@	BOS	Danny MacFayden	t 1	
130/134	49	9/7/1927	@	BOS	Slim Harriss	t 8	
134/138	50	9/11/1927		SLB	Milt Gaston	b 4	
135/139	51	9/13 (Game 1)		CLE	Willis Hudlin	b 7	
136/140	52	9/13 (Game 2)		CLE	Joe Shaute	b 4	
139/143	53	9/16/1927		CHW	Ted Blankenship	b 3	
143/147	54	9/18 (Game 2)		CHW	Ted Lyons	b 5	
144/148	55	9/21/1927		DET	Sam Gibson	b 9	
145/149	56	9/22/1927		DET	Ken Holloway	b 9	
148/152	57	9/27/1927		PHA	Lefty Grove	b 6	
149/153	58	9/29/1927		WSH	Hod Lisenbee	b 1	
149/153	59	9/29/1927		WSH	Paul Hopkins	b 5	
150/154	60	9/30/1927		WSH	Tom Zachary	b 8	

SOURCES

Books

Alexander, Charles C.: *Breaking the Slump: Baseball in the Depression Era*. Columbia University Press, 2002.

Appel, Marty: *Pinstripe Empire: The New York Yankees from Before the Babe to After the Boss*. Bloomsbury, 2012.

Auker, Elden (with Tom Keegan): *Sleeper Cars and Flannel*. Triumph Books, 2001.

Benson, Michael: *Ballparks of North America: A Comprehensive Historical Encyclopedia of Baseball Grounds, Yards and Stadiums, 1845 to 1988*. McFarland Press, 1989.

Boxerman, Burton A. (and Bonita W. Boxerman): *Jews and Baseball, Volume 1: Entering the American Mainstream, 1871–1948*. McFarland Press, 1989.

Carlisle, Rodney P. (edited by): *The Great Depression and World War II 1929–1949* (Handbook to Life in America Series). Facts on File, 2009

Cottrell, Robert C.: *Two Pioneers: How Hank Greenberg and Jackie Robinson Transformed Baseball—And America*. Potomac Books, 2002.

Detroit News: *They Earned Their Stripes: The Detroit Tigers All-Time Team*. Sports Publishing, 2000.

Dorfman, H. A. (and Karl Kuehl): *The Mental Game of Baseball: A Guide to Peak Performance*. Diamond Communications, 2002.

Ephross, Peter (with Martin Abramowitz, edited by): *Jewish Major Leaguers in Their Own Words: Oral Histories of 23 Players*. McFarland Press, 2012.

Falls, Joe: *The Detroit Tigers: An Illustrated History*. Walker & Company, 1989.

Greenberg, Hank (with Ira Berkow): *Hank Greenberg: The Story of My Life*. Times Books, 1989.

Foer, Franklin (and Marc Tracy, edited by): *Jewish Jocks: An Unorthodox Hall of Fame*. Twelve, 2012.

James, Bill: *The New Bill James Historical Baseball Abstract*. The Free Press, 2001.

Jones, Gerard: *Men of Tomorrow: Geeks, Gangsters, and the Birth of the Comic Book*. Basic Books, 2005.

Kennedy, David M.: *Freedom From Fear: The American People in Depression and War, 1929–1945*. Oxford University Press, 1999.

Klima, John: *The Game Must Go On: Hank Greenberg, Pete Gray, and the Great Days of Baseball on the Home Front in WWII*. Thomas Dunne Books, 2015.

Kurlansky, Mark: *Hank Greenberg: The Hero Who Didn't Want to Be One*. Yale University Press, 2011.

Kyvig, David E.: *Daily Life in the United States, 1920–1940: How Americans Lived Through the 'Roaring Twenties' and the Great Depression*. Ivan R. Dee, 2004.

Levine, Peter: *From Ellis Island to Ebbets Field*. Oxford University Press, 1992.

Marrus, Michael R.: *The Unwanted: European Refugees in the Twentieth Century*. Oxford University Press, 1985.

McCollister, John: *The Tigers and Their Den: The Official Story of the Detroit Tigers*. Addax Publishing, 1999.

Mead, William B.: *Low and Outside: Baseball in The Depression*. William B. Mead. Redefinition, 1990.

Megdal, Howard: *The Baseball Talmud: The Definitive Position-by-Position Ranking of Baseball's Chosen People*. Harper, 2009.

Ritter, Lawrence: *The Glory of Their Times*. Harper Perennial, 1992.

Rosengren, John: *Hank Greenberg: The Hero of Heroes*. New American Library, 2013.

Ruttman, Larry: *American Jews and America's Game*. University of Nebraska Press, 2013.

Shlaes, Amity, *The Forgotten Man*. Harpercollins, 2007.

Sommer, Shelley: *Hammerin' Hank Greenberg: Baseball Pioneer*. Calkins Creek, 2011.

Stewart, Wayne (edited and introduced by): *The Gigantic Book of Baseball Quotations*, Skyhorse Publishing, 2007.

Sullivan, Dean A. (compiled and edited by): *Middle Innings: A Documentary History of Baseball, 1900–1948*. University of Nebraska Press, 1998.

Surdam, David George: *Wins, Losses, & Empty Seats: How Baseball Outlasted the Great Depression*. University of Nebraska Press, 2011.

US Bureau of Census: *Historical Statistics of the United States: Colonial Times to 1970, Part 1*. 1975.

Film/Documentary

The Life and Times of Hank Greenberg, 1998, directed by Aviva
  Kempner, The Ciesla Foundation.

Websites

Aish.com
Baberuth.com
Baseball-reference.com
Baseballguru.com
digitalcollections.nypl.org
ESPN.com
Forward.com
Hardballtimes.com
RooseveltInstitute.org
TheAtlantic.com
volokh.com

Newspapers and Magazines

Altoona Tribune
Asbury Park Press
Baltimore Sun
Brooklyn Daily Eagle
Boston Globe
Boston Jewish Advocate
Chicago Sentinel
Chicago Tribune
Christian Science Monitor
Cleveland Plain Dealer
Collier's Magazine

Daily Jewish Forward
Dearborn Independent
Deseret News
Detroit Free Press
Detroit Jewish Chronicle
Hartford Courant
Los Angeles Times
New York Herald Tribune
The New York Times
Newsweek
Pittsburgh Post-Gazette
Rochester Democrat and Chronicle
The Sporting News
St. Louis Post Dispatch
St. Louis Star and Times
Time
Washington Post

ACKNOWLEDGMENTS

There are a number of people who deserve credit for any project like this, since no writer is an island.

I would like to thank my editor, Jason Katzman, for offering me the opportunity to tell this particular "chapter" in the life of Hank Greenberg. Whether you think he was the victim of anti-Semitism or just a victim of circumstances, it was an education not only to learn about what Hammerin' Hank went through, but what the country and the world had to deal with in those uncertain times.

Thanks to Stuart Shea, who took on the arduous task of proofreading the book. His great "defense" (that is, making good catches) saved me no small measure of potential embarrassment.

Thanks to John Rosengren, author of the excellent biography, *Hank Greenberg: The Hero of Heroes*, and Ira Berkow, who crafted the Hall of Famer's memoirs, *Hank Greenberg: The Story of My Life*, for their unselfishness in providing extra insight.

My gratitude to Matt Rothenberg, manager of the Giamatti Research Center at the National Baseball Hall of Fame and Museum, who graciously endured countless interruptions in his daily routine to answer questions and provide suggestions for material that greatly improved the project. And another hat tip to John Horne in the Hall's photo archive department.

A note of appreciation also goes to my wife, Dr. Faith Krausman, for putting up with my long hours and hand wringing.

And finally, thanks to the encouragement of all those out there who expressed their interest and memories of what Hammerin' Hank meant to them.

INDEX

R

S

T

Temple, Shirley, 24, 87
Treder, Steve, 173
Trosky, Hal, 77, 90, 161
Tye, Larry, 71
Tyson, Ty, 7

V

Vander Meer, Johnny, 64, 68, 84, 134
Vidmer, Richards, 56–57, 133–134, 161

W

Wade, Jake, 6, 28, 36
Walker, Dixie, 24, 27, 115
Ward, Arch, 76
Ward, Charles P., 8, 32, 36, 62-63, 67, 70, 72-73, 77, 91-93, 96, 110, 116-118, 132–133, 138, 140, 142, 150
Wheaties, 66, 93, 126

White, Jo-Jo, 27, 53–54
Whitehead, John, 20, 211–212, 216, 218
Whitehill, Earl, 140, 153, 208, 213, 217, 220
Wilson, Hack, 4, 140
World Series, xxiii, 1-4, 94, 76, 138, 163, 172, 185,
World War II, 140, 166–170, 172–174, 177, 185–186
Wulf, Steve, 101

Y

Yom Kippur, 3, 147–148
York, Rudy, 8, 32-33, 40-44, 46-47, 57, 61, 63–64, 66–69, 73-76, 78, 90, 95–96, 113, 153, 161

Z

Zeller, Jack, 41